THE GOD OF THINNESS

THE GOD OF THINNESS

GLUTTONY AND OTHER WEIGHTY MATTERS

Mary Louise Bringle

ABINGDON PRESS
Nashville

THE GOD OF THINNESS
GLUTTONY AND OTHER WEIGHTY MATTERS

Copyright © 1992 by Abingdon Press.

Library of Congress Cataloging-in-Publication Data

Bringle, Mary Louise, 1953–
    The god of thinness: gluttony and other weighty matters. / Mary Louise Bringle.
        p.   cm.
    Includes bibliographical references.
    ISBN 0-687-148278   (alk. paper)
    1. Gluttony.   2. Body, Human—Religious aspects—Christianity.   3. Food—Religious aspects—Christianity.   4. Bringle, Mary Louise.   I. Title.
    BV4627.G5B75   1992   91-42502
    241'.3—dc20   CIP

CONTENTS

ACKNOWLEDGMENTS

A number of people have "fed" me in important ways during the process of writing this book. Seven students at St. Andrews Presbyterian College took part with me in an experimental course on "Feasts, Fasts, and Food Addictions," in which I began a systematic exploration of these ideas: Candi Cann, Bill Daniels, Beth Green Fellenstein, Sylvia Mebane, Shannon Miller, Faith Thompson, and Tim Ward. I am grateful for their insights, support, and good humor. Scores of women have subsequently participated in workshops I have conducted on issues of food and body image; their stories and struggles have urged me to keep writing.

Letha Dawson Scanzoni, researcher extraordinaire, vied with my mother, K. Harrison Bringle, for top honors in sending me useful clippings and articles on food and diet. My mother and father, Emmett Bringle, both provided unparalleled proof-reading expertise. Rex Matthews of Abingdon Press plied his editorial skills with customary efficiency and finesse.

Tom Benson supported me invaluably, both as Dean of St. Andrews, which granted the sabbatical leave during which this project was accomplished, and as a non-size-obsessed friend, who took away my digital bathroom scale (to which, good riddance!). Mel Keiser, of Guilford College, offered much-needed reassurance on matters both personal and academic. Jerry Godard, also of Guilford, read or heard every word of the manuscript, some of which first took form in letters to him. For such patient prompting from such significant companions, the only conceivable acknowledgement is, "Thank you."

Finally, important appreciation belongs to Shirley Arnold, who shares my table and tolerates my eating idiosyncracies, to Cinda, and to Elmo the Ample, who purred in my lap while I word-processed every page (and who mysteriously gained every pound I lost during the course of writing).

Sweeter is all such sustenance than honey: yea, and more deeply fulfilling, too.

Laurinburg, NC
August 1991

Frozen Yoga

The ice cream is softening to room temperature. Around the inside edges of the carton, it is already liquefying to a voluptuous custard. I stand at the kitchen counter, a silver teaspoon in hand, and scoop up the most melted mouthfuls from the corners of the box. I am not actually eating, mind you; I am redecorating, transforming a block of unevenly thawing ice cream into an oval of uniform consistency. This is important work. If the ice cream which has melted around the edges is put back into the refrigerator in that condition, it will probably refreeze in unappetizing lumps. I therefore commit myself to this task of corner custard-extraction as a favor to any future ice cream eater. (It is irrelevant at this juncture that I am the only ice cream eater in my household; there are always potential guests to consider.)

After ten minutes or so of work, the oval looks about right; the margins between ice cream and carton reach to an even three-eighths of an inch on all sides, with appropriately rounded corners. A new problem arises, however. Ice cream is softening at an alarming rate all across the exposed top surface of the box. I begin scraping it off, carefully, down to the rock solid portion below. If my strokes are smooth enough, they leave an even, almost virginal surface; in fact, the back of the spoon does an admirable job of glossing over the rough edges, those tiny peaks and valleys that appear as a result of scraping. This part of the

9

re-decorating job is like icing a cake. It is not merely important work; it is an art form.

But every artist must cope with the particularities of her medium. Wood has its knots; marble, its veins. This ice cream has *things* in it: small squarish bits of fudge, and chips of pecan. Such *things* never congregate in the corners or along the outer surfaces of the box. They don't even sink to the bottom. I know this, because in my efforts at uniform melt-removal I have more than once turned an entire block of ice cream upside-down in order to scrape its lower extremities to an even match with its upper. No: by the centripetal miracle of modern ice cream packaging, all the *things* distribute themselves toward the middle. (Or perhaps this is not such a technological miracle after all, because the middle also seems to be where ice cream chunks prefer to distribute themselves in the human body which has consumed them. Perhaps there is something of an Aristotelian teleology involved.)

At any rate, the appearance of *things* interferes with the achievement of a uniformly smooth surface. I will be gliding the edge of my silver teaspoon with dexterous artistry across the ice cream oval, removing the last vestiges of its liquefying layer . . . and then, bump! A *thing*. I suppose a person who was inclined to tolerate imperfections might simply leave it there, jutting its chunky head up from the surface, like a rock partially buried on a playground. I am not so tolerant. I know rocks can be dangerous, and I have a Petrine determination to complete with thoroughness any task I have undertaken.

Excavation is the only answer. Truth to tell, I suspected there would be *things* in this ice cream. After all, I am the one who selected this patently chunky flavor from my grocer's dairy case. But the packagers could have made a mistake, accidentally or deliberately; they could have neglected to stir *things* into this particular half-gallon. As a scholar, I am trained in a hermeneutics of suspicion; when it comes to food packaging, one can never be certain that the contents will match the claims of the label.

Digressions and distrustfulness notwithstanding, there *are* indeed *things* in this ice cream. And I have come properly equipped for excavation. A silver teaspoon works best—preferably a family heirloom, with edges worn paper thin. A stainless steel spoon is

10

too cumbersome; it gouges the surface. One might as well use one's fingers. (Hideous thought: I shudder even to imagine it.) A plastic spoon is too iffy, the handle too likely to break at a recalcitrant chunk. An ice cream scoop is unthinkable; this is, after all, surgery, not demolition. No: a burnished silver teaspoon is the optimum instrument.

Properly equipped, I begin my archeological extractions. A chocolate chunk here, a pecan chip there. It is difficult to know when to desist from such operations. The silver spoon slices neatly, removing just the pebbles and leaving the surrounding earth intact, as it were; leaving tiny, well-spaced holes, as if the ground has been efficiently aerated. But the goal of this enterprise was (wasn't it?) the achievement of a uniformly smooth surface. I seem to be getting farther and farther from my objective. The process of mining for chocolate and pecans has taken on momentum of its own. I wonder now if I can rest before all offending intruders have been removed from the creamy whiteness of the carton?

This is hard work. I know it is, because I can begin to feel an ache between my shoulder blades. I have not stood up straight for the past half hour. To do so would disturb my concentration, make it harder to see the shadows of irregular chunks beneath the ice cream surface, make the trajectory from spoon to mouth all the more laborious. I am hunching and digging and scraping and smoothing and putting ice cream coated morsels over and over into my mouth. The sheer repetitiveness of the ritual is mesmerizing, a kind of soft-frozen "yoga." The sugar in my bloodstream and the rhythm of my movements are combining to make me drowsy. But it would take more effort to stop what I am doing than to keep on going, keep on relentlessly scraping and smoothing, digging and redecorating.

Or, to be perfectly honest, *eating*. Eating compulsively. I push the carton away, and find myself in tears.

◆　　◆　　◆

Thomas de Quincy wrote his nineteenth-century confessions of an English opium eater. My confessions as an ice cream eater are perhaps less grandiose. But they are painful—and I am begin-

11

ning to think that perhaps they are important. They are important to me as a woman and a compulsive eater and a theologian. I have wondered about the appropriate ordering for those identifications. Am I a woman with an eating problem who just happens to be a theologian; or a theologian with an eating problem who just happens to be a woman; or a feminist theologian who just happens to have a problem with food?

All of these descriptions make a certain sense, but I think it is the first one which is the most accurate. My primary sense of myself is that of being a woman who has struggled all her life with issues of food and diet and body image. Spread on top of that identity, as it were—icing on the cake, marmalade on the toast—is a layer of theological education. But these images are not quite accurate, for they keep the ingredients of my selfhood too distinct. So sample this instead: my tendencies and training in theological reflection are like a lemon sugar glaze poured over the warm sponge cake of my identity as woman and compulsive eater, such that the tart sweetness seeps into every pore, mingling flavors into a single, multi-seasoned delectation. Appetizing? Well, yes, much of the time. But also potentially hazardous to the health. Oh, not the literal hazards of eggs and butter and sugar. Rather, I mean the metaphorical hazards of mingling womanhood and eating compulsions with theological questioning. Sometimes it may be better for my mental and emotional health not to think too much about such things. Sometimes it would at least be more comfortable to keep theological reflections out of the path of my daily activities. Theology should, after all, be done in the study, the library, the office—should it not?—and not at the kitchen counter. Theology should be done hunched over a Bible (or a newspaper, or both—thank you, Mr. Barth), and not over a half-gallon of Butter Pecan Fudge ice cream.

But theology has seeped into my pores. So even when I have literally anaesthetized myself with carbohydrates (triggering the release of soothing serotonin in my brain); even when I have dulled my rational thought processes with rhythmic, repetitive, ritual activity—even at such moments, the theological questions keep rising. Sometimes they are primitive in expression: "My God, what am I doing?" This may not sound as eloquent as the

Psalmist's lament: "Out of the depths, I cry unto Thee!" But anyone who has shared the experience knows that both outcries are similarly heartfelt.

Sometimes the questions are more sophisticated in phrasing. At what point have I crossed the line between legitimate enjoyment of the fruits of the creation and illegitimate abuse of those gifts? When I am attempting to "undo" a round of compulsive eating by a spate of compulsive dieting, have I brought my behavior into any better line with religious ideals of responsible stewardship? Is there a culpable dimension to my compulsive eating behavior: Is it an example of willful perversion, of what used to be condemned as the deadly sin of *gluttony*? Or does my behavior (and that of so many other eating disordered people in contemporary western societies) show me to be an unfortunate victim: of abnormal endorphin-enkephalin metabolism; of high-sugar, high-fat food processing; of the advertising wiles of a consumer culture? What do my preoccupations with food and weight say about my personal system of values; what do they say about the values at large of an affluent—and addictive—society? Are my eating and dieting patterns relevant to my religious life—or are they somehow too mundane, too trivial, to merit theological attention? Do the ways I feed (or mis-feed) my body have any impact at all on the ways in which I nourish my spirit? If issues of spirituality as well as corporeality are at stake in my eating habits, then are there spiritual resources which might be fruitfully engaged in the processes of recovery from food addictions?

Current responses to such questions sound with something of a confusion of tongues. As seems so often the case, the most dissonant voices come from the fundamentalist right and the feminist left. Voices from the right proclaim that *obesity* itself is sinful; that overeating is a tool of Satan. "Does the devil want you fat?" one such author inquires. Yes, indeed, he answers. Satan smacks his lips at the prospect of overweight Christians who are ruining their health, shortening their lives, disobeying God's word, lacking in self-control. "Christian weight control classes" present the solution. A prayerful, Bible-based lifestyle will enable believers to "get God's help in losing unwanted pounds."[1]

There is certainly some wisdom to this position. If I had the spiritual maturity to live my whole life as a prayer, I doubt I would find myself seeking to fill the empty spaces inside me with morsels of Butter Pecan Fudge ice cream. Insofar as the ingestion of such morsels clogs my bloodstream with sugar and butterfat, it does threaten my health and defile the "temple of the Holy Spirit" which is my body.

On the other hand, however, the voices from the right sound a bit simplistic in their suggestion that "overweight" itself is the problem, and that dieting (even "biblically-based dieting") is the solution. Numbers of binge eaters are not, in fact, overweight; numbers of people whose weight exceeds the actuarial "ideals" eat with relative moderation. Dieting can take on an obsessive life of its own: witness the sometimes fatal excesses of anorexia nervosa and bulimia. To understand the dynamics of destructive eating, we must look not only at the sinfulness of the individual eater, prey to self-will and the wiles of Satan; we must also examine the social, political, and economic realities of a society which places such premiums on consumption and on the cosmetics of "body image."

Voices from the feminist left do a better job of taking into account the societal factors ingredient in weight-related issues. Radical feminists active in the Size Acceptance movement challenge the claims that being fat is itself either sick or sinful.[2] "Weightism," or discrimination against people based on their physical size and shape, discloses dynamics of prejudice which are intricately interwoven with classism, sexism, and heterosexism. Perhaps, the Size Acceptance activists suggest, our goal should not be the obsessive re-shaping of our individual bodies, but rather the re-shaping of society into a more pluralistic appreciation of the many shapes and sizes in which human bodies come.

Again, there is much to be learned from this position. If I could simply let my body *be*, celebrating its distinctiveness rather than agonizing over all the ways in which it does not "fit" the cultural ideal, I would lose the composite sense of shame, guilt, and self-hatred that lurks behind so many compulsive eating episodes. "For every diet there is an equal and opposite binge," writes the feminist Geneen Roth, and bitter experience attests to

14

the truth of her equation.[3] To cease dieting (whether that diet be based on the gospel according to Stillman, Tarnower, Atkins, Edelstein, or whomever, or purportedly based on the Bible itself) is to engage in a socially subversive and revolutionary act, and an act of self-liberation.

Still, even if fat itself is not the problem and if dieting itself *is* more the problem than the solution, there nonetheless remain ways in which my eating (and that of so many like me) represents cause for legitimate concern. When I am hunched over a half-gallon of Butter Pecan Fudge ice cream (or a bag of potato chips or whatever a particular binge food might be), I *know* I am doing something self-destructive. Even if I fast the rest of the day to keep my caloric intake in balance; even if I run ten miles to "undo" the excesses of the binge; even if I return immediately thereafter to healthier habits of nutrition; even if (which is potentially most important) I refuse to scourge myself into self-loathing for my moments of compulsive indulgence . . . *even so*, I know in my gut (both literally and metaphorically) that I have *sinned* against God, and against me.

The word *sinned* sounds harsh—perhaps especially so to feminist ears which are more attuned to the compensatory modern language of self-celebration than to the traditional moral language of self-censure. Nevertheless, I use it deliberately. I am reluctant to point accusatory fingers at myself or at anyone else who is suffering (and binge-eating *is* suffering, despite its pleasurable appearance to the contrary). I am more than reluctant to indict people whose body size suggests (perhaps incorrectly) that their eating is out of control. However, I do recognize in my own experience that habits of compulsive eating (and of compulsive not-eating) stand as signs of a fundamental brokenness and alienation. I recognize that feeding myself with frantic mouthfuls of food can be a way of swallowing down emotions and seeking to flee some uncomfortable truth about myself. I recognize that obsessing about calories consumed or expended can be a way of worshiping the cultural "god of thinness," deflecting my devotion from the One True God.

Thus, the feminist voices seem ultimately lacking to me in their short-shrifting of the seriously sinful dimensions of eating behavior; and the fundamentalist voices seem lacking in their focus upon Satan and self-will to the exclusion of any other dimensions of the problem. But out of this confusion of tongues, perhaps the most strident voice of all sounds in the *silence* of mainstream ethicists and theologians on issues of food, weight, and diet. Such silence seems to imply that it really does not matter how I feed or mis-feed my body as long as my spirit is well-nourished: clearly a docetic distortion! Such silence implies that personal concerns about health and well-being are inferior to social concerns about feeding the poor.

But the point is that such issues are not ultimately separable from one another. The ways that I am in my body both ground and reflect the ways that I am in my spirit and in the world. I can enjoy or abuse the fruits of the creation; I can be a good or a wasteful steward. I can be gluttonous or generous with the gifts of divine abundance, enlisting them in the service of what is ultimately valuable, or squandering them in the pursuit of some idolatrous value. Theological silences notwithstanding, such matters are far from trivial. They have to do with the wholeness and the holiness of my daily existence, which has to do with nothing less than the ways I can devote myself to the grace-filled work of helping God's will to be done on earth, as it is in heaven.

Jesus taught us to pray that we should be given our daily bread; he also taught us that we do not live by bread alone. Jesus fasted in the wilderness for forty days to prepare for his ministry; he also exhorted the disciples to feast while the bridegroom was in their midst. In these dialectical teachings lie the essential ingredients for "cooking up" a Christian theology of eating. They present us with a recipe which we can ill afford to file away, untested. For they may well be the recipe for recovery after which our food-addicted selves, and our addictive society, have been most deeply hungering.

Milk and honey, bread and wine, a few ripe figs out of season, and the fellowship of friends around a table: in such ingredients, literal and symbolic, both our bodies and our spirits are fed. Better by far are such pleasures than the solitary and furtive indulgence of Butter Pecan Fudge ice cream—or any other food eaten frantically without tasting, eaten numbly beyond the point at which one has reached one's fill. There are rituals more sustaining than the anaesthetic and frozen "yoga" of shoveling a spoon from carton to mouth and back again. This book proposes to seek out such pleasures, and to integrate them into a creation-centered, incarnational, Christian theology. The questions posed in this *apéritif* have set the table before us. So, "Here let us feast, and to the feast be join'd / Discourse, the sweeter banquet of the mind."[4]

    Bon appétit!

Food for Thought

SO WHAT?

I awoke this morning to self-hatred and a carbohydrate hang-over. Last night before bedtime, I systematically ate an entire box of granola. If you or someone you care about can sympathize with the two previous sentences, keep reading. If not, stop now.

I struggled all day yesterday, the first official day of my first official sabbatical, to keep my foodlife under control. It was not easy. Instead of the rhythmic distractions of classes, committee meetings, appointments with students, and encounters with colleagues on campus, unpeopled and unstructured time stretched out blankly before me. Food—which I refuse to keep in my office at school (for obvious reasons)—signaled its constant availability from the kitchen cabinets, a mere six steps away from the desk in my study at home. I struggled to ignore the signals. I worked diligently, taking notes, sorting note cards, organizing files of sources and ideas in all those preliminary ways that serve as a prelude to—or a procrastination from—actual writing. I succeeded fairly well at keeping myself busy and at not overeating until about 10:00 p.m.

I'm not quite sure what happened at 10:00 to trigger the eating episode. Perhaps fifteen waking hours was as long as my psyche felt like submitting to the duress of restraint. Perhaps some deep nerve center finally registered my resolve that the time had come to quit the procrastinating preliminaries and to start putting my own words onto paper. Perhaps apprehensiveness over the prospect of getting up the next morning and staring at a blank computer screen sent me scrounging for carbohydrates: to dull the anxiety; to guarantee a good night's sleep; to insure that I would be so groggy today that I could not possibly expect myself to work creatively at the computer keyboard?

Or perhaps to give me something about which to start writing. I am not above noticing the ironic aptness of this situation—or even the humor. Last fall, while anticipating my sabbatical, I more than once caught myself wondering whether or not I would be able to refrain from overeating while sitting at home writing a book on the dynamics of overeating. The bizarre fittingness of such queries struck me as funny. Even this morning, now that two cups of black coffee and two loads of clean laundry have assisted in easing my self-hatred, I find myself amused by the pertinence (or impertinence?) of my own behavior patterns. Prior to last night's granola extravaganza, I had not binged in several months. Perhaps some unconscious part of myself decided to give me a pointed "come-uppance," to remind me how bingeing and its aftermath feel.

I do believe in the existence of such unconscious wisdom within myself. The more I become conscious of its presence and promptings, the more I find myself moving from pathology toward healthiness in my long-problematic relationship with food. The account of this slow healing process will be important in subsequent chapters of this book (particularly Chapter Four). For now, it seems important to note that the same internal wisdom which did not want me too "uppity" about my own recovery as a compulsive overeater also did not want me too "abstracted" in my writing about it. Instead, it sent me an experience which pressed to be narrated in the first person.

In fact, I had been deliberating for months over what voice to use in writing this exposition: how "scholarly" and "objective" to attempt to be, how personal or autobiographical. While the former voice frustrates me with its occasional pedantry, the latter voice frightens me with its inescapable proximity. It is scary to begin a sentence by writing the simple words, "I am." It is particularly scary to complete such a sentence by confessing, "I am a compulsive eater," because a key ingredient in that very pathology is its furtiveness, the fact that it is undertaken in hiding. It is even scarier to write "I am a compulsive eater" in a book intended for the theology rather than the "self-help" counters of local bookstores. My gut fear is that some fellow theologian will pick up this volume, read the opening confession, and curl his lip in the responding question, "So what?" (I say "his" deliberately, because I fear this retort more from men than from women—for reasons which will become clear later on, if they are not intuitively apparent already.) I suppose it is my own protectiveness about such responses that prompts me, in the first paragraph of this chapter, to request that a person simply stop reading if he or she is unable to sympathize with the phenomenon of awakening hung-over and self-hating after an episode of binge eating.

In essence, though, the remainder of this chapter constitutes an effort to respond to the "So what?" question. I am a compulsive eater and dieter; I awoke this morning to self-hatred and a carbohydrate hang-over. So what? So, for one crucial matter, I know I am not alone. To judge from statistics about eating behaviors in the United States today, there are thousands upon thousands of people who also woke up this morning feeling "fat," feeling the need to embark on a diet after the indulgences of the recent Christmas holidays, or feeling self-hatred for having already failed at the diet which was undertaken with New Year's resolve just a few days ago. (For other seasons of the year, other phrases can be substituted: the indulgences of a recent vacation, family celebration, personal consolation; the dietary resolve of a new week, new month, new relationship, new job.) An initial response to the "So what?" question thus entails an examination of the *significance* and *scope* of food and diet-related issues: their significance not only in terms of the numbers of people who share such problems, but also in terms of the volume of material resources which we as a culture invest in the creation, perpetuation, and attempted cure of food addictions, and the amount of attention and energy which we as individuals direct (or misdirect) toward our food lives and fatness phobias.

Even a substantial case for the significance of eating problems in contemporary culture, however, may not satisfy the "So what?" question of the lip-curling theologian. Granted that many Americans who are fortunate enough to live above the poverty level may in fact eat "not wisely, but too well." Still, why should anyone attempt to discuss such a behavioral aberration in a work of *theology*? Perhaps there are *ethical* ingredients to the problem: resources squandered on the diet industry by wealthy North Americans in a world in which poverty-stricken masses die every minute of malnutrition; food left, physically or metaphorically, on our prosperous plates, while children in other parts of the world—or even in our own neighborhoods—are starving. Let the ethicists, then, continue calling us to more responsible eating habits, to more ecological and political sensitivity regarding the morally appropriate *Diet for a Small Planet*. But what has any of this to do with theology?

I confess that as a theologian I have asked this very question of myself on more than one occasion. If theology is a discipline that concerns itself with ultimate questions about the nature and workings of the sacred, then doesn't it have more important matters to consider than the systematic consumption, in a single sitting, of a ten ounce box of granola? Haven't I taken a bit of a leap from the sublime to the merely *silly* when I move from issues of the salvation of suffering humanity, in the here or the hereafter, to issues of the satiety or insatiability of my own stomach?

It is embarrassing to put the issue so bluntly. But I am beginning—based once again on the promptings of an internal wisdom—to suspect that such embarrassment is a cover, a mask, a defense mechanism. I am beginning to suspect that what we as human beings most *trivialize* is what we most *fear*. Certainly, the past three decades of equal rights activism have amply demonstrated how the belittling of women's experiences serves as an attempt to suppress feminist threats to entrenched patriarchal power. Similarly, the belittling of food-related issues serves its own attempt at suppression. But suppression of what?

At this juncture, the "So what?" question seems to me to move onto firmly theological ground. Because what I suspect is at issue in the obsession with food and diet matters in the United States today, and what is equally at issue in their omission from serious theological treatment is—for lack of a better phrase—a new gnosticism.[1] Gnosticism of any stripe or any era represents an attempt to achieve salvation through secret knowledge (*gnosis*) which is available only to the initiated few. Gnosticism also represents an attempt to achieve such salvation through a flight from the disgusting encumbrance of the physical body. It is easy to see how dietary fetishes illustrate a new gnosticism: repulsed by the onus of flesh, of fatness, of our own frantic appetites, we turn to the salvation promised by the esoteric wisdom of the latest diet formula. It is perhaps less easy to see how theological neglect of such issues itself constitutes a gnostic perversion. But what is it if not gnosticism when we whisper to ourselves that our daily dietary behaviors do not *matter*; that what *really* matters theologically is the *transcendent*: the sacred, the sublime, and not the mere *stuff* of our stolidly embodied existence?

Like it or not, though, it is the very stuff of bodiliness which our eating behaviors urge us to ponder (which literally means to "weigh"). And what better arena in which to ponder such matters than Christian theology? Because Christian theology, once relieved of its gnostic propensities, locates the sacred *not* in some remote seventh heaven, but rather here on earth: in the flesh of incarnation, in the body and blood of bread and wine, in the table fellowship of those whose common cause is to feed the God embodied within "the least of these."

The Christian theologian thus has three important fronts on which to answer the "So what?" question about the attention-worthiness of compulsive eating and its kindred behaviors. The first, already mentioned, is the general, sociological issue of the *significance* and *scope* of the problem: the numbers of people involved and the quantity of resources (of money, attention, and energy) invested in it. The second and third fronts are more specifically theological. In capsule form, they have to do with the *symbolics* and *sacramentality* of Christian faith, on the one hand, and with the resultant *spirituality* of Christian life, on the other. In slightly less abbreviated phrasing, they have to do with the challenge to concoct a fittingly *juicy* Christian theology of creation and incarnation, and with the corollary charge to cultivate a sensuously

23

responsible (or responsibly sensuous) practice of daily Christian living.

THE SCOPE AND SIGNIFICANCE OF FOOD-RELATED PROBLEMS

On the mornings when I wake up feeling "fat" and hating myself for it, I can take some slim comfort in knowing that at least I am not alone. The scope of food and diet-related problems in the United States today is (with apologies for the seemingly unavoidable infelicity) enormous. As early as 1973, one year before "anorexia" became a household word in this country, researcher Albert Stunkard noted that "interest in obesity almost assumes the dimensions of a national neurosis."[2] In the two decades since his pronouncement, with an increasing incidence of eating disorders and a continuing spread of weight preoccupation to broader segments of the U.S. population, this neurosis has only intensified. What was once a predominantly WASP-waisted cult of slenderness grew in the 1970s and 1980s into an equal opportunity obsession: a Gallup Poll conducted during this time period discovered that 41% of nonwhites thought of themselves as overweight.[3] What was once the particular self-perfecting province of adult women became a self-conscious concern in the lives of young girls as well: a 1986 study in the San Francisco and Chicago areas found that from 50%–80% of fourth grade girls were on diets.[4]

These ten-year-old girls were simply following the popular trend. On any given day, an estimated 65 million Americans are dieting.[5] In addition to the fourth graders, this number comprises nearly two-thirds of the female high school population, not to mention the millions of adult men and women who are informally "watching what they eat" or formally following some fixed diet program.[6] The enormous and escalating statistics in and of themselves are telling: on what else would such a diverse cohort of 65 million Americans be able to agree, except on the presumption that they are all "too fat"? But what may be even more significant than these numbers is the set of perceptual distortions lurking beneath them: a phobia about fatness (fully two-thirds of adult women report in response to surveys that one of their greatest worries is over getting fat); an inaccurate and injurious body image (nearly 95% of adult women overestimate their body size; 75% of adults within the "ideal" range of weights for their heights still think they need to be thinner).[7]

What is merely a national neurosis when it concerns the fat phobia and diet mania of most weight- and waist-watchers becomes a matter of pathology when it concerns the increasing numbers of people (predominantly women) who are afflicted with eating disorders. While surveys and statistics vary slightly, the generally calculated population of anorexics—individuals who are systematically starving themselves to death in the "relentless pursuit of thinness"—is placed between 5% and 10% of all American girls and women. And the phrase "starving themselves *to death*" is no exaggeration: the American Anorexia and Bulimia Association (AABA) reports that each year 150,000 American women die of anorexia—as many as 19% of those who are hospitalized for the disease. To put this number into sharper perspective, Naomi Wolf points out that "there are 17,204 more deaths from anorexia in the United States every twelve months than the total number of deaths from Aids [*sic*] tabulated by the World Health Organization in 177 countries and territories from the beginning of the epidemic until the end of 1988."[8]

While the mortality rate is lower, the rate of incidence is much higher for the eating disorder of bulimia (occasionally termed "bulimarexia" or "the binge-purge syndrome").[9] As many as one-third of all female college students are thought to engage in the habitual use of laxatives, vomiting, and diuretics in order to rid their bodies of unwanted food and weight. Women above college age, and even a small percentage of men (particularly those whose professions force weight-consciousness: jockeys, dancers, wrestlers) also binge and purge, though not in the concentrated numbers of the female college-age population.[10]

Once again, younger children are not exempt from such potentially hazardous behaviors: a 1987 report to the U.S. House of Representatives, Select Committee on Children, Youth and Families disclosed that over 10% of 15-year-olds induce vomiting as a means of controlling weight.[11] While less frequently fatal than anorexia nervosa, bulimia can also be carried to life-threatening extremes; short of death, it can induce electrolyte imbalance, heart damage, perforation of the stomach, rupture and bleeding of the esophagus, rectal bleeding, anemia, amenorrhea, and even erosion of tooth enamel from the acidity of frequent vomiting.

In short, significant numbers of young people and adults in the current U.S. population are affected in significant ways by diet-related disturbances. If population percentages alone are not enough to justify a theological exploration of eating problems, the amount of money invested in such problems solidifies the grounds for legitimate concern. On an episode of "60 Minutes" early in the 1980s, Mike Wallace made the staggering claim that "More dollars are spent on worthless cures for obesity than for all medical research combined."[12] Testimony before recent Washington hearings by the House Subcommittee on Regulation indicate that the diet industry earned $33 billion in 1989.[13] Sociologist Barry Glassner reports that the dollar figure skyrockets to $50 billion when it expands to include cosmetics, plastic surgery, health clubs, and fitness gadgetry.[14] Historian Roberta Pollack Seid has computed a statistic with peculiar pertinence to those of us who are interested in both food and theology: that "sales of diet books outrank sales of all other books on the market, except for the Bible."[15]

It is not far-fetched at all to suggest—as do numerous commentators—that dieting has assumed the fervor and proportions of a leading new "religion" (albeit a gnostic one), with its own bible, its own ritual observances, and its own high priestesses and priests. Involving millions of people and billions of dollars, this national religion of dietary righteousness also merits attention for its impact upon the less tangible resources of our attention and energy. Something dramatically important is being said about the values of our society when a preponderance of women over sixty report that "gaining weight" is their "second most serious concern" (after a concern over memory loss); when a physician and a psychologist can adjure us that "the number on [the] scale [is] the most important number in your life"; when 42% of respondents to a poll say that they would rather lose ten or fifteen pounds than find success in their relationships or careers, and nearly 40% say that what they *fear most in this world* is "getting fat."[16] If religion has to do with the state of being "ultimately concerned" (in the words of Paul Tillich's well-known definition), then the figures about our figure-consciousness show us to be pouring our money, our energies, and ourselves into a "religious" pursuit of the pseudo-ultimate concern of thinness.

Perhaps such statistics about the scope of food-related problems will begin to satisfy the lip-curling theologian that compulsive eating and dieting are significant phenomena in our culture which warrant serious attention. Some people do find numbers helpful and convincing. Others among us, though, are well aware of the "fudge factor" in figures. Compulsive dieters, in particular, know the devious ploys which statistics invite. We know how to manipulate the insurance company tables of ideal weights by calculating ourselves at large rather than medium frames, by measuring our height while wearing "two-inch heels," but immediately removing those heels before stepping onto the scales. We know how to make our scales register down a notch by positioning them carefully along the fault lines of our bathroom floors. We know that half a cantaloupe has fifty calories (all our diet bibles confirm this), so we search through the produce section of our grocery store until we find the one closest to a basketball in circumference—and we compute its caloric value as if it were of regulation softball size. We grudgingly count up the calories of whole cookies (when we allow ourselves to eat them), but conveniently assume that broken pieces and crumbs have had their fattening properties leaked out through the breakage. If you don't do any of these things yourself, I am willing to bet that you know someone who does. The compulsive eaters and dieters among us know that numbers can lie, because we make them do so with daily regularity. And it would all be rather amusing—if it weren't all so painful.

For behind the statistical scope of eating problems lies a personal toll which is far more significant, if far harder to calculate. To speak of awakening to self-hatred the morning after a carbohydrate binge is not to be melodramatic. Other voices than mine will attest to this fact; perhaps the classic one belongs to the woman whom existential psychiatrist Ludwig Binswanger named "Ellen West." His case study of her treatment for a weight loss obsession, in the early years of this century, cites this poignant lament: "This is the horrible part of my life; it is filled with dread. Dread of eating, dread of hunger, dread of the dread."[17] Ellen West: my sister, my friend! Indeed, it can be horrible: to dread eating, to dread not eating; to wake in the morning with the fear of not being able to make it through the day without losing control; to wake in the morning with the heartsinking sense that a life so tightly controlled is not really worth living anyway; to fear companionship because it so often centers around food, which means temptation; to fear solitude because it so often leads to a frantic attempt to stuff down the ache of emptiness with anything edible—which then leads to a feeling of numbness, of failure, of self-loathing. What makes it all worse is to recognize with trenchant clarity, in the very midst of these preoccupations, the pettiness of such concerns. In a world where people are dying of starvation, how utterly stupid—how utterly obscene!—to be driven to despair by the prospect of eating a few hundred calories "too much," of gaining a pound or an inch or two.

With this trenchant recognition, it becomes tempting to enter into yet another turn of the vicious spiral, and to loathe oneself (myself, ourselves) for such self-loathing. But I strongly suspect that to take this turn is to join the lip-curling confederacy of those who trivialize what they fear. I readily grant that food- and diet-obsessions show my personal values and our nation's cultural values to be askew. Still, I equally readily claim that to discount these obsessions—to feel guilty for harboring them and to attempt to move on quickly to other "more important" things—is to become an unwitting initiate into the ranks of the new gnosticism. I no longer believe in a gnosticized gospel of salvation by trivialization. Rather, I believe and affirm that the flesh *matters*; that food *matters*; that hunger and satiety and the accompanying dread of both emptiness and abundance *matter*. Indeed, from a Christian perspective, all these things matter profoundly: not just for their personal poignancy, but also for their rich theological resonance with the grounding symbols and sacraments of the faith.

THE SYMBOLICS AND SACRAMENTALITY OF FOOD IN CHRISTIAN FAITH

The Christian scriptures themselves are marbled with food: milk and honey, bread and wine, pomegranates and figs, fatted calves and grilled fish, Paschal suppers for small gatherings of friends and miraculous picnics for multitudes. The symbolic narrative of Christianity opens in an earthly garden of delights and closes with the heavenly marriage supper of the Lamb. In the beginning, God creates a material world and calls it "Good!" At the decisive juncture of the story, God takes on human flesh in order to dwell within that very creation. While in the flesh, God in the person of Jesus of Nazareth is so fond of sharing meals with friends and enemies alike that he is labeled a "glutton and a drunkard" (Mt. 11:19; Lk. 7:34). How could anyone attend to this narrative in all its full-bodied flavor and come away with the impression that what and how we eat does not matter?

Food and fleshliness matter. Without food, we do not live at all; without good food, we do not live as abundantly as we might. If life itself is a gift, then eating shows us how that gift both requires and receives renewal on a regular basis. Between the ages of twenty and fifty, each one of us spends roughly twenty thousand hours—more than eight hundred days, over two full years—in the process of eating.[18] Yet, this very regularity prompts us to forget the deep significance of what we are doing. The daily graces are the ones which we are most inclined to take for granted. Writes M. F. K. Fisher, food critic and gastronomic philosopher:

> Too few of us, perhaps, feel that the breaking of bread, the sharing of salt, the common dipping into one bowl, mean more than the satisfaction of a need. We make such primal things as casual as tunes heard over a radio, forgetting the mystery and strength in both.[19]

Yet, eating *is* a primal mystery: as mysterious as sex (about which much more seems to get written); as mysterious as the preciousness and precariousness of life itself. Perhaps prosperity has so sated our stomachs that we have grown insensitive to this mystery. In his preface to Piero Camporesi's study of *Food and*

Fantasy in Early Modern Europe, Roy Porter reminds us that such insensitivity is a luxury of relatively recent origins:

> We live today in a society in which the eating of bread has become a dietary irrelevance. . . . Precisely the reverse was true in pre-modern times. Bread marked the divide between life and death. . . . Making, breaking, and distributing bread carried profound connotations of friendship, communion, giving, sharing, justice—indeed, literally, companionship.[20]

Those of us who are fortunate enough to live in a culture of affluence need such reminders. Not only do we need the ethical reminder that an equitable distribution of bread, of all food, is a *sine qua non* of justice. Further, we need the *theological* reminder that the consumption of bread, of all food, stands as a sacrament of our fundamental dependence: on the source and ground of our existence, on the earth, on our own fleshly bodies, and on one another.

Food and God

A "heuristic" or metaphorical theology of food requires an image of God, the ground of our existence, as Feeder—an image which runs rampant throughout the symbolic texts of Christianity.[21] Not only is God the giver of food: the provider of manna and quails in the wilderness, the multiplier of loaves and fishes on a mountainside. God Godself becomes food, offering God's own body and blood in the sacramental bread and wine of the eucharist. Medieval iconography portrays this vividly: a believer stands beside the Crucified One, holding a chalice in which to catch the nutritive blood which flows from Jesus' side, from a wound placed curiously, tellingly, where a mother's breast would be.[22] Holy Mother Jesus; Holy Nurturing God! Such symbolism is not accidental. As vulnerable, hungering creatures, we know that food is our primordial need. Without physical nurture, regularly given, both our bodies and our spirits wither. Eating is a metaphor both of our ongoing vulnerability and of God's ongoing activities of creation and sustenance.

Yet, food is not merely our primordial need; it is also our primordial pleasure. A theology of food reminds us not only that our lives are precarious, dependent on mysterious sources of sustenance which we cannot clearly control. Such a theology also reminds us that our lives are precious, graced with delights both simple and profound. Even as I write this paragraph, I am in the process of baking shortbread for a friend whose husband is ill. The house is rich with the smell of butter, subtly scented with almond extract. Such smells call vividly to mind (No: not just to mind; to embodied mind, to fleshly mind) that life as God's gift is not about *mere* being. It is about *well*-being, blessed being: about abundance and renewal, sensuousness and sabbatical refreshment. It is about the seasoned care which good food serves forth. A theology of food is perforce a theology of gratitude and of giving. It is also, palatably and palpably, a theology of joy.

Food and the Earth

If a metaphorical theology of food begins with the symbolism of God as Feeder—nurturing mother, sacramental self-giver, providential provider—it moves irresistibly on to a symbolics and sacramentality of the earth as the medium through which food is given. To view the creation as food is perhaps to invite misunderstandings—anti-ecological images of the earth as mere prey for human despoliation. Such images, however, serve to show how insensitive we have become to the mutual dependence and delight to which an attuned theology of eating recalls us.

Even from a utilitarian perspective, a theology attuned to eating calls us to realize that we cannot have good food if we despoil the land. The Hebrew roots of our Christian faith should teach us this much. In the creation narrative in Genesis 2, the earth creature is placed in the Garden of Eden with orders "to till and keep it." Both verbs are respectful ones: the verb translated "till" (*'bd*) also means to serve; the verb for "keep" (*shmr*) emphasizes protection, not possession. In her exegesis of this narrative, Phyllis Trible summarizes the mutual dependence of the earth creature and the rest of the creation:

> Botany and humanity are one in origin and in substance: God made them both from the ground. Their harmony is also hierarchy: botany serves humanity; humanity preserves botany. The garden

provides aesthetic pleasure [and] physical nourishment. . . . Yet the earth creature has no license to plunder and exploit it. It must revere the soil.[23]

If there is a hierarchy between the human creature and the earth which is created to supply its food, this hierarchy nevertheless requires mutuality and care. Therefore, even as God the Creator rested on the seventh day, so the human steward of the creation is to observe, every seventh year, "a year of solemn rest for the land" (Lev. 25:4).

Such utilitarian respect for the earth as the source of sustenance is only the beginning of a theology oriented around the symbolics of eating. For such a theology must surely move beyond a utilitarian understanding of food to a sacramental and celebrative one. The person who simply "eats to live" may well be missing a crucial point: that eating is intended to be a voluptuous, and not simply a functional, activity—and that stewardship of the creation is not just about mutual dependence: it is also about delight.

No one develops such insights better than Robert Farrar Capon in his inimitable theologico-gastronomic chefs-d'oeuvre, *The Supper of the Lamb* and *Food for Thought: Resurrecting the Art of Eating.* Capon insists that the whole motive force behind the divine creativity is joy: God creates the earth not because it is useful or necessary, but because it is desirable. Consequently, human beings—acting *in imago dei*—are called to relish the creation, not for its utility, but for its intrinsic pleasingness. "Earth is not convenient," Capon says; "it is good." By extension:

> Food does not exist merely for the sake of its nutritional value. . . .
> A [person's] daily meal ought to be an exultation over the smack
> of desirability which lies at the roots of creation.

This "smack of desirability" is something which we not only discover but we also, in our own priestly fashion, enhance. "Seasoning," for Capon, becomes "a sacrament," an act in which we lift the creation higher toward that Ultimate Delight which was its origin and which will be its end. To eat well, to season and sacramentalize and celebrate our eating, can restore to us a "sense of the festivity of being."[24] To see being as "festive" can teach us to treat the earth with ecstasy rather than exploitation.

Food and Our Bodies

What applies to the earth as God's creation applies equally to our own bodies. Again, the Hebrew roots of Christianity prove instructive. Our gnosticized Christian dualism between the fettering flesh and the unfettered spirit is foreign to the Hebraic depths from whence we spring. Matthew Fox reminds us that Jewish spirituality is "so undualistic" that the Hebrew language does not even contain a separate word for body and for soul. The Hebrew distinction is between the "living person" and the "deadening or disspirited person," not between a disembodied spirit and an encumbering (and abuse-inviting) body. Fox quotes Hebrew Bible scholar Gerhard von Rad in concluding that, for the Wisdom of Ancient Israel, "our bodies and passions and all creation blessings" are "thoroughly worthy of trust."[25] If we trust our bodies as both precious and precarious gifts of their Creator, then they too invite us to abandon exploitation in favor of ecstatic festivity.

Such an invitation is keenly important in a culture which appears to be as cavalier about abuse of the human body as it is about abuse of the natural world (as if the two could ever be legitimately separated). So much of what and how we feed ourselves is abusive. In a book on *Attitudes to the Body in Western Christendom*, Frank Bottomley has suggested that "perhaps a more significant sign of modern attitudes to the body may be seen not in [our] attitude to nudity or sex but to food."[26]

Indeed. Our new gnosticism is showing. Perhaps nowhere does our gnostic body-hatred appear more clearly than in our correlated eating extremes. Overindulgence or underindulgence: on the one hand, food laden with fats and sugars, crammed into our mouths at all hours of the day and night while we stand at a kitchen counter or hunch at a desk or slouch behind the wheel of an automobile; on the other hand, food stripped of real calories, re-processed with fake fats and fake sugars, picked at with finicky precision while we attempt to discipline, deny, and otherwise subdue our bodies into slender subjugation. Overindulgence or underindulgence, stuffing or starving: neither of these extremes is actually attuned to the body's basic needs or basic pleasures.

THE GOD OF THINNESS

Feminist psychotherapist Susie Orbach has labeled "the anorectic's struggle" a "metaphor for our age."[27] I wonder. I think
bulimia—bingeing and purging, overindulging or underindulg-
ing—supplies a more accurate metaphor.

Or perhaps that is simply because bulimia has been my personal affliction, and therefore I know it better. I know fat phobia
and flesh hatred from the inside out: know the dread of eating
and the dread of not eating, know the horrors of feeding myself
frantically and then fasting or vomiting or exercising to exhaustion or abusing diuretics and laxatives in order to avoid the
seemingly-worse horror of gaining so much as a pound. If this is
not abuse and exploitation of the body, what is? My problem, the
bulimic's problem, our culture's problem in general is that we
either oversacralize or undersacralize (desacralize, desecrate) the
flesh. We make it into an idol—the perfect body, the sacred icon
toward which we all aspire and in the religious pursuit of which
we expend vast amounts of money and energy and attention. Or
else we make it into a demon—the obstinate body which refuses
perfection, and which we therefore must exorcize (and exercise)
into submission. We have lost a sense of balance; we have lost the
sense that the body itself is neither sacred nor execrable. Rather,
the body is a gift from the sacred, through which the sacred may
become palpable, through which we may reach toward the festivity and ecstasy which lie at the heart—in the very marrow, the very
juice and joy—of being.

This balanced perspective applies to my own body—which I
must learn (and am gradually learning) to love and to trust in due
measure, to celebrate as a locus for sacred enfleshment: for
incarnation. It applies also to the bodies of other people. If there
is one overarching attitude to which a metaphorical theology of
food calls us, it is that of appreciating variety. The earth which is
given as food to be tended and respected, seasoned and shared,
comes forth from the Creator as a garden filled with variegated
delights. God's creation teems with diversity: bodies and beings
abound in all shapes and sizes. It is *man*-made [only minimally *sic*]
products that seek a plastic uniformity. We blaspheme the divine
creativity when we self-righteously assume that there is only one
acceptable size or shape for a human body to be!

Granted, not all the gifts of divine abundance are equally fit for food, and there are things which we as stewards and priests of the creation can do to make some of them more (or sadly, less) fitting. Granted, not all bodies in their abundant diversity are equally healthy, and there are things which we as stewards and priests of our own fleshliness can do to make our bodily lives more (or again, sadly, less) healthful. Still, it is a far cry from stewarding to subjugating, and a far cry from seeking "fitness" to sneering at physical configurations that deviate in the slightest degree from an idolized cultural norm. "Fittingness" is not the same thing as conformity or uniformity. Some bodies are designed to be fleshier than others; some bodies are appropriately rounded and softened rather than hardened and angular. The key note of a metaphorical theology of food should be not censure but celebration: a respectful appreciation of the manifold ways in which we receive the sacrament of life in the flesh.

Food and One Another

Appreciation of bodily diversity is but one theme with interpersonal implications which emerges from a theology oriented around the metaphors of food and eating. At an even more basic level, eating reminds us of our inescapable interdependence. Not only does the precariousness and preciousness of our life itself depend upon a mysterious, steady, nurturing source. Not only are we dependent upon the earth and upon our own fragile and festive fleshliness. We are also born into this world—and remain for as long as we live in this world—keenly dependent upon one another.

We are born into this world dependent, fed *in utero* by the body and blood of our mothers, fed *ex utero* by the milk and care of those who tend us. Often again, these tenders are mothers. The associations between femaleness and feeding are strong ones, grounded in biological processes of pregnancy and lactation and sutained by social and political expectations of maternal child care. From this dual basis, elaborate symbol systems have arisen to link women with food and flesh in distinctive ways. Women become not only the feeders of infants, but the feeders of whole families of humanity. Women become not only the source of our biological birthing, but the very emblem of our dependent embodiment. Food comes to be psychologically, symbolically equated with female power, the awesome power to give or withhold nurture. Through a series of frightened patriarchal reactions to this power, women's social roles become further and further restricted until food remains as one of the few media through which female competency and creativity can reach expression.[28]

Is it any wonder that out from under this biological, sociopolitical, psychological, and symbolic freight, women emerge as particularly troubled by issues relating to food, feeding, and body size? Is it any wonder that the traditionally male enterprise of theology has trivialized or totally ignored these issues for so very long?

Food is a human issue, to be sure; but it is preeminently—at least in contemporary American culture—a women's issue. When I conduct workshops on food and body image, I ask participants to try to envision a culture in which roughly 40% of men and virtually no women would be afflicted with eating disorders of one kind or another. While I would not want to create such a culture (turning tables is ultimately no more gratifying than setting and clearing them over and over again), I find responses to this exercise revealing. In general, they describe a society in which men would be set at war with their bodies: by being given high fat to muscle ratios and slow metabolisms (not to mention pregnancies), making it easy for them to gain weight and difficult for them to lose it again; by being made into sexual objects whose access to physical and emotional security would depend upon a slender appearance; by having to provide food for others yet deny it to themselves for fear of becoming "fat" (which would translate into "undesirable," outcast, powerless); by suffering all the rebound effects of deprivation (leading to a vicious cycle of compensatory indulgence, followed by self-hatred and more attempted compensation and consolation through self-feeding).

The picture of such a dystopian culture is not a pleasant one, but it is painfully familiar to thousands upon thousands of women in the United States today. In an article on "Body Hate" in a recent *Ms.* magazine, Dalma Heyn summarizes our current situation:

Our phobia about fat, our revulsion at looking female . . . are a
scandal. Yet . . . we are too embarrassed . . . to recognize a women's
issue when we see one. We prefer instead to battle our own intrinsic
femaleness, to beat our bodies into the shape our psyches insist
on. . . . We have become our own worst enemies, perpetrators of
anti-femaleness without even knowing it.[29]

Other voices as well (Kim Chernin, Susie Orbach) articulately
analyze the relationship between our cultural gnosticism—our
disgust at fleshliness—and our cultural misogyny.[30] When we hate
rounded and softened bodies, when we spend our money and
energy in the quasi-religious pursuit of muscled hardness and
angularity, a large part of what we are hating is our native
femaleness. And, to return to our origins (in more ways than one),
what we are hating about femaleness is its relentless reminder of
our interdependence and vulnerability.

As human creatures—creatures molded of *humus*, creatures
born of *mater* and matter, of woman and earth—we are inescapably
interdependent. "Macho" attempts at invulnerable individualism
notwithstanding, we can neither eat nor *live* unless we tend and
let ourselves be tended in turn by the earth, by our bodies, and
by one another. The grounding symbols and sacraments of Christianity make this plain. Carl and LaVonne Braaten summarize
such symbolism admirably in their slender volume on *The Living
Temple: A Practical Theology of the Body and the Foods of the Earth*:

> The message of salvation on which Christianity rests comes to us
> in a sacrament of flesh (Jesus), a sacrament of water (baptism), a
> sacrament of food (bread), a sacrament of drink (wine), and a
> sacrament of persons (joint members of the body of Christ).[31]

As joint members of one body, created in the image of a God who
is Creative Nurture and Holy Food, we are called to the festivity
of table fellowship and to the ministry of mutual feeding. We are
called not simply to "say grace" together as we sit down to our
daily rituals of eating, but actually to *be grace* together as we share
with one another the fruits of the land, of our labors, and of the
loving bounty of God.

If such are the orienting symbols and sacraments of our
heritage, then there are clear implications for answering any "So

what?" question about the significance of eating behaviors within Christian theology. The frantic bingeing and purging of the bulimic, the compulsive fasting and exercising of the anorexic, and the preoccupied calorie-counting of the chronic dieter all point to distorted relationships: distorted relationships with the earth and the body as well as with their ultimate sustenance in the Creator and their penultimate sustenance in the care of fellow creatures. Disordered eating defies the companionship (the literal "bread-withness") for which we were created. Bingeing, purging, fasting, and obsessive dieting and exercising are primarily private activities; they promote withdrawal from rather than engagement in community. It is hard for me to love my neighbor when I am constantly measuring the shape of my body against hers, or envying his ability to eat with impunity, or despising her lack of self-discipline, or wishing he would leave the house so that I could "get at" the contents of the refrigerator unobserved. It is hard to give genuine hospitality when my energies are consumed in a spiral of dread: dread of eating and of not-eating; dread of control and of loss of control. It is hard to celebrate the interdependence of fellow creatures when I am caught in an excruciating cycle of distrust and yearning: distrust that anyone will be ever able to love me as I am, with all the flaws that seem glaringly manifest in my own body's "imperfections"; yearning that somehow, something, someone will come to fill up all my lonely, hungry, aching, empty spaces. Eating disorders offer both a profound exemplification and a powerful metaphor for the disruption of human relatedness in general, because they embody that disruption at the level of the most basic symbols of our co-humanity: sharing milk and breaking bread together.

When I cannot, or do not, or will not eat with my fellow creatures—or when, conversely, I cannot or do not seem to be able to stop eating—I am bodying forth the brokenness of a fallen world and of a distorted will (though not of an intrinsically evil *body*; these distinctions will continue to appear). Not only am I refusing and defying companionship; I am also refusing the carnal medium through which gifts of grace appear. God created embodied beings and called them good; God hallowed the human body with God's own incarnation; God feasted with friends *and enemies* and bids us do likewise; God invites us to the wedding supper of the Lamb. Such are the foundational symbols of the Christian story. In the light of such symbols, both underindulgence and overindulgence, both the deliberate denial of appetite and the insensible stuffing of appetite beyond satiation stand out with starker meaning. Both extremes of our eating behavior make manifest our sinfully frightened resistance to savoring that "smack of desirability" in the creation, of which Robert Farrar Capon speaks. Both extremes show how acutely we need to elaborate the symbols and sacraments of our Christian heritage into a concrete spirituality: a spirituality which will teach us better to serve and to savor God's grace in the most basic activities of our daily living.

THE SPIRITUALITY OF EVERYDAY LIFE

Perverse though it sounds—indeed, perverse though it be—we *are* fearfully resistant to savoring grace. While it may be more blessed to give than to receive, there are clear occasions for many of us when it is also *easier*. Receiving can be difficult; accepting a gift, a joy, threatens the boundaries of our small securities. Pleasure can be overwhelming: genuinely *ec-static*, it takes us outside ourselves, sets us "beside ourselves," propels/impels/compels us to look at the world from a novel perspective. A surprising and overwhelming pleasure thwarts our habits of measuring out our lives in units of merit: this much we have earned . . . no less, but also—anxiously—no more! It is hard for us to receive what we have not deserved, because such receiving forces us to the humility of recognizing that we are, in fact, generally undeserving. We do not deserve our precious and precarious lives; we do not deserve the radical gift of our being or the superadded gifts of our well-being. Such matters come to us as grace. Yet, we attempt to limit the graces we will receive and so retain at least a pretense of control. We would rather make our own lives too small than let ourselves be dwarfed—even by the magnitude of divine generosity.

Different people experience this resistance to grace and generosity in different ways. Some people mask and manage it better than others; a person with an eating disorder masks it poorly if at at all. I remember vividly the first time I read Susie Orbach's book, *Fat Is a Feminist Issue*. In that book, she describes a fantasy exercise which affected (and still affects) me profoundly. She asks the reader to imagine having unlimited leisure time and money to spend, and taking a trip to a supermarket. She continues with these instructions:

> Take a couple of supermarket carts and fill them up with all your favorite foods. . . . Be sure not to skimp. . . . If you like cheesecake, take several, take enough so you feel that there is no way you could possibly eat it all in one sitting. . . . Cast your eyes over the wonderful array of foods and fill up your cart. . . . [Take all the food to your home]. . . . Bring the food into the kitchen and fill up the room with it. . . . How do you feel surrounded by all of this food just for you?[32]

I must confess that my gut reaction to this fantasy is one of utter *terror*. I do not know what to do in the midst of such abundance. I feel a panicky desire to throw all the food away, or simply to flee. In trying this exercise with other eating disordered people, I have found that they react in a similar fashion. The question is, Why? The answer, I think, taps not simply into personal pathology, but into theology as well.

Elaborating a theological answer to this question invokes a number of interwoven themes, some of which we have already visited, and most of which we will revisit in subsequent chapters: fear of unworthiness (just mentioned), as well as the closely related fear of loss of control; fear of hunger and emptiness, closely tied to a frantically compensatory and ultimately frustrating pursuit of self-satisfying satiation; a puritanical suspicion of pleasure, correlated with a gnostic distrust of the body; an absolutizing inability to distinguish nuances of difference between legitimate enjoyment and illegitimate hedonism, or between appropriate discipline and inappropriate ascetic extremes. All these themes point together to our need for a developed spirituality—a set of everyday rituals and practices which will teach us how to deal more wisely with our hungers and our pleasures, a set of practices which will help us to be sensuously responsible and responsibly sensuous in our appropriation of the gifts and graces of our corporeal and corporate living.

Hunger and Satiation

Hunger is a both a primal experience and a profound metaphor of the human condition. We hunger after food as we hunger after meaning, after relationship—or, on our blessed days, after righteousness. It is only minimally metaphorical when we speak of the satisfaction of any our ends as a full/fill/ment: the inner urge which keeps us yearning after all manner of "goods," including the greatest good of all, *feels like* a yawning emptiness in search of filling. Augustine, coiner of the phrase *cor inquietam* to describe the heart that is restless until it finds its rest in God, also sees the close relationship between such restlessness and the experiential metaphor of hunger. In his work *On the Usefulness of Fasting*, he writes:

> When people are hungry, they stretch out toward something; while they are stretching, they are enlarged; while they are enlarged, they become capacious, and when they have become capacious enough, they will be filled in due time.[33]

Our hungers show us our capaciousness as well as our neediness, and invite us to stretch beyond ourselves toward a source of possible satisfaction.

It is precisely this stretching, however, which can be so frightening. When I reach out for something, there is always the threat that it will not be there when I want it and that I will come away empty-handed. The assurance that my hungers "will be filled *in due time*" is no guarantee that they will be given instant gratification. The uncertainty of waiting makes me anxious. Rather than live with the anxiety of emptiness, I seek to full/fill myself with whatever comes most readily to hand.[34] The more that lies at hand, the more frantic I may become. This is one reason Susie Orbach's fantasy exercise evokes such terror: I see myself in the overstocked kitchen, stuffing down every delicacy in sight as I try to satiate my urgent hunger: a hunger that stretches toward a source of fulfillment which lies ultimately outside my control; a hunger that no food can ever truly satisfy.

Puritanism and Distrust

Perhaps it is the very urgency of hunger which prompts the gnostic to distrust the body and the puritan to be suspicious of its pleasures. Both hunger and pleasure can threaten our equilibrium, drawing us toward irrationality, impulsiveness, excess, ecstasy. Both can tempt us to idolatry, creating mini-gods and pseudo-ultimates out of whatever stimulates or sates our senses. Both can bind us to immediate satisfactions and blind us to needs and values beyond the present moment. There are real dangers to which the gnostics and the puritans alert us. We should give their wariness due heed.

Still, there is a difference between due heed against bodily pleasures run riot and deep distrust of bodily pleasure altogether. In one of her collections of essays on food, M. F. K. Fisher tells a story which aptly illustrates the latter extreme:

> Once when young Walter Scott . . . was exceptionally hungry and said happily, "Oh, what a fine soup! Is it not a *fine* soup, dear Papa?," his father immediately poured a pint of cold water into what was already a pretty thin broth. . . . Mr. Scott did it, he said, to drown the devil.[35]

I have to wonder. When we pour cold water, literally or metaphorically, over the gifts of the creation, are we boldly "drowning the devil," or are we blasphemously drowning out the voices of genuine gratitude and celebration? (Jesus, after all, did not water down his wine; rather, he "wined up" his water!)

Indulgence and Asceticism

The key issue for a de-gnosticized, im-puritanized Christian spirituality becomes one of making distinctions: between when the body and its inner "wisdom" deserve our trust and when they demand our suspicion; between when the pleasures of the flesh invite our indulgence and when they should invoke our discipline. Such distinctions are neither universal nor absolute: one person's self-awareness may be another's self-deception; one's simple pleasure may be another's provocation to painful excess. Some people can sense when their bodies are crying out for rest or touch or movement; other people mistranslate all such yearnings into a desire for food. Some people can eat half a bowl of ice cream and be satisfied; others eat a few spoonfuls and cannot seem to stop before consuming half a gallon. This diversity in our degrees of attunement to our needs and appetites demands that we shape personalized guidelines to differentiate between irresponsible and responsible sensuousness. In so shaping, we participate in a long-standing spiritual tradition. As Margaret Miles reminds us: "A Christian life may be much more one of self-conscious, ongoing alertness to the need for correcting one's particular propensities—'temptations,' historical Christians called them—than a matter of discovering universal prescriptions, equally useful and pressing on everyone who undertakes to live as a Christian."[36]

The processes of such alertness and self-correction traditionally fall under the rubric of "ascesis"—a term with both helpful and hurtful connotations in the history of Christian thinking. Technically, *asceticism* refers to a program of training, making the whole self "fit" for God's service; indeed,the desert ascetics of the early church were known as "great athletes."[37] As such, asceticism does not denigrate or distrust the body as do gnostic and puritan dualisms. Rather, the ascetic trades on the holistic connection of the body and the spirit: the training of one inseparably enhances the health of the other; the proper ordering of bodily impulses provides energy for the pursuit of ultimate desires. Miles instructively cites the *Homilies* of Gregory Palamas, a fourteenth-century Eastern Orthodox theologian:

> If the body is to partake with the soul in the ineffable benefits of the world to come, it is certain that it must participate in them as far as possible now. . . . For the body also has an experience of divine things when the passionate forces of the soul are not put to death but transformed and sanctified.[38]

Genuine asceticism, then, does not seek to kill the passions but rather to learn from them and lift them to greater wholeness and holiness.

There is a profound sense, therefore, in which genuine asceticism serves as the ally, not the enemy, of sensuous indulgence. The trained body is more appreciative of its pleasures. Occasional deprivation cleanses the palate; temporary renunciation sharpens senses which tend to grow dull from excessive use. Hunger is, after all, the best seasoning, and sweets taste even sweeter after the deprivations of Lent. Attention to what and how we feed ourselves, to when and how we experience our various bodily hungers, can thus work to make us more *responsible* in a dual sense: not only can it make us more maturely *accountable for* the gifts of our living; it can also make us more keenly *responsive to* them.

Such holistic and helpful connotations of *ascesis* fall under sociologist of religion Max Weber's rubric of "inner-worldly asceticism," a positive valuing of life in this world that seeks the salutary ordering of impulses. Weber contrasts this category with that of "other-worldly asceticism," a devaluing of this world which attempts to deny or destroy all earthly desiring.[39] More often than not, however, it is asceticism of the "other-worldly" variety which we have in mind when we hear the term. The hurtful connotations of such world-rejecting *ascesis* invite abuse of rather than appreciation for the body. The anorexic stands before us as a stark (literal as well as figurative) example of this kind of gnostic orientation. Whether she starves herself in the pursuit of sanctity (as with the "holy anorexics" of the medieval era)[40] or in the pursuit of a secularized ideal of perfection, she is attempting a rigid control—indeed, a dualistic conquest—of the flesh: a *mortification* which can lead, all too literally, to death.

Because of its hurtful connotations, even Margaret Miles—historical scholar of Christian *ascesis*—has abandoned earlier attempts to "rehabilitate" the term, deciding that "asceticism" itself is "the name of a pervasive internal misinterpretation of Christianity, a word that invites, if not entails, a dualistic disdain for bodies and the natural world."[41] In its place, she chooses to talk about attentive *practices*: "individual and communal practices of self-discipline based on self-knowledge"; "exercises, carefully chosen and individually tailored to address a particular person's compulsive behavior, addictions, or destructive thought patterns."[42] From Miles's perspective, even those exercises which entail physical deprivations, such as fasting, are not undertaken as a means of mortifying the flesh. Rather, they are undertaken as a means of vivifying the whole self, flesh and spirit, focusing the energies of the one in order to enhance the vitality of the other.

In making her terminological choice, Miles is akin to Matthew Fox who prefers to speak in his "creation-centered" spirituality not of asceticism, but of *discipline*. Fox reminds us that the word "discipline" comes from the word "disciple"—one who is "allured or attracted by another," one who chooses to commit time and energy to learning more from the other's company.[43] To "disciple" myself to Jesus is to attend with care to his lifestyle and his teachings; to "disciple" myself to a musical instrument is to spend countless hours rehearsing techniques until they become as comfortable as second nature; to "disciple" myself to my body is to tune in to its promptings, learning to discern its various pains and hungers and its levels of genuine satisfaction and pleasure. To practice discipline is not to punish myself but to promote my total well-being—even when such promotion demands intense effort, rigorous self-examination, humble attention to the insights of others, and occasionally stringent sacrifice.

Indulgence and discipline, therefore, are not polar opposites of one another (as indulgence and "other-worldly" asceticism can be). Rather, they are paradoxical complementaries. To heighten my care about what and how I eat is to increase, not diminish, my pleasure in eating; to savor my pleasures is to train, not distract, my attentiveness to God's creation. As Matthew Fox observes, "If we savored more . . . we would be less compulsive, less unsatisfied."[44] As any self-conscious bulimic knows, it is precisely our patterns of underindulgence that set in motion our compensatory overindulgences; it is our frightened and puritanical self-denials that set us up for binges later on. The bulimic's problem, my problem, our cultural problem, is that we think more easily in absolutizing extremes than in nuances of difference: either binge or purge, either all or nothing, either utter hedonism or utter abstinence.

Either sensuousness or responsibility. But the wisdom of a creation-centered Christian spirituality lies in the nuanced and paradoxical middle: in an attitude of sensuous responsibility and responsible sensuousness—an attitude which indulges with care in order to become a more disciplined "disciple," and which sacrifices with joy in order all the more keenly to "taste and see that the Lord is good" (Ps. 34:8).

Rituals and Practices

How can we learn the wisdom of this paradoxical middle ground? How can we learn to taste, to savor in disciplined ways, the goodness of God's creation? Those of us who are fearful of grace and anxious about abundance stand particularly in need of responses to such questions. In particular, we need the help which rituals and practices can provide in training us toward a more sensuously responsive spirituality.

Such help is as regularly present as our daily activities of food preparation and food consumption. Yet we tend to overlook these key resources for our spiritual lives, and we do so for a variety of reasons. In part, our reasons root in our gnosticism: our dualism between the flesh and the spirit, which extends into a dualism between the secular and the sacred—a dualism which forces our literal daily meals into a subordinate position below our symbolic weekly (or quarterly) acts of communion. In part, our reasons root in our sexism: our trivializing sense that what women (predominantly) do in the kitchen and dining room as feeders of our own bodies is significantly less important than what men (predominantly) do in the sacristy and the sanctuary as feeders of the body of Christ.[45]

We need to break through such dualisms. Once we begin to do so, we can see that every act of eating is a sacrament—a sacrament, as I said earlier, of our fundamental dependence on the source and ground of our existence, on the earth, on our own fleshly bodies, and on one another. If all eating is sacramental, then all eating should call us to an attitude of reverent delight—an attitude which it is hard to maintain while either deliberately starving or indiscriminately stuffing our bodies.

To recognize the value of such an attitude and to act it out habitually, however, are two different things. No one knows this discrepancy more keenly than the person with an eating disorder. What may be simple for someone with a "normal" relationship to food can be alarmingly difficult for an anorexic, a bulimic, a compulsive overeater or a chronic dieter. People in these categories find themselves (ourselves) in the odd position of having to *learn* how to do what other people do naturally: namely, to eat. In the process of such learning, a variety of "practices" (in Margaret Miles's terminology) come into play. We will return to look at these practices more closely in discussing the process of recovery from eating disorders in our final chapter. At this juncture, however, what is important is to name them and to note their rootage in a longstanding spiritual tradition. What is important is to establish conclusively for the confederacy of lip-curling theologians that issues of food consumption genuinely *matter* for Christian theology. Three such "mattering" practices are feasting, fasting, and "fine-tuning" of the self.

The fact that we do not ordinarily think of feasting as a spiritual discipline shows how seriously our understandings have been distorted by a puritanical distrust of pleasure and a gnostic focus on "other-worldly" asceticism. But if "to discipline" means (after Fox) "to become a disciple," then *Christian* discipline enjoins us to enjoy the creation: while the disciples of John the Baptist fast, the disciples of Jesus celebrate with food and drink the presence of their Beloved (Mt. 9:14-15). The Christian calendar defines a number of feast days whose purpose is to regularize and ritualize the practice of rejoicing in the present, palpable, and palatable graces of God.

Despite superficial similarities, a feast is not the same as a binge: in fact, it is very nearly the opposite of and antidote for bingeing. Feasting entails loving preparation of food and table, reenacting the *imago* of the divine creativity; bingeing involves a heedless and destructive hand-to-mouth frenzy. Feasting cries out for fellowship; bingeing hides in isolation. Feasting savors every flavor, texture, aroma; bingeing rapidly becomes anaesthetized and insensate. Frantic eating numbs the palate and the spirit; we do not notice the tastes of food or the signals of satiation from our own bodies. Because we are not really tasting it, no amount of devoured food can satisfy us. And so, we consume more and more, but enjoy it less and less. Bingeing hurts. Feasting, on the other hand, delights. When we practice feasting, we learn to savor as well as to sense our limits of pleasurable fullness. In so doing, we learn a visceral lesson in the complementarity of self-indulgence and self-discipline.

If feasting puts us in touch with the pleasures of food and of our bodies, fasting serves in a correlated way to heighten our sensitivity. Not only does it sharpen our physical appetite; it can sharpen our moral appetite as well. Fasting makes us feel in our guts (both literally and metaphorically) the reality of suffering and the brokenness of a world in which starvation coexists with supersatiation. Perhaps more than any other practice of self-discipline, fasting reminds us of our radical dependence. To fast is to surrender control of our own feeding temporarily in order to trust—in Augustine's words—that we will "be filled in due time."

Just as a feast is very nearly the opposite of a binge, a fast is very nearly the opposite of a diet. Both fasting and dieting limit food intake, to be sure—but they do so in dramatically different ways. The diet (at least, the weight-loss diet, which is the primary connotation of the word in contemporary usage) entails *willful* restriction; we speak admiringly of the dieter's presumed *will power*. The fast, on the other hand, involves a willing relinquishment of power. As James Massey notes in his discussion of *Spiritual Disciplines* in the biblical and early Christian communities:

> Fasting . . . deepens in the whole self a sense of . . . dependence upon the strength of God. Fasting is more than an act of abstinence. It is an affirmative act; it is a way of waiting on God; it is an act of surrender.[46]

When we fast, we enact the trust that we do not have to fill all our own hungers in the present moment; rather, we rely on a future in which God will provide. Where a weight-loss diet prompts us to focus our attention on ourselves (checking and re-checking the scales, the tape measure, the mirror, to see if we have become any more "attractive," any more socially acceptable), a fast takes our mind off ourselves and off our cultural idols, and allows us to think on other things. Where a food-restriction diet perversely prompts us to focus our attention on food (either painstakingly computing what we are permitted or obsessively hankering after what we are denied), a fast takes our mind off food altogether. Where a diet confines, a fast sets free.

So feasting and fasting are time-honored practices within the history of Christian spirituality which help to counter our disordered attitudes toward food. The fact that the liturgical calendar sets aside specific days for both kinds of "discipline" offers us a needed insight into the rhythm of our living. As finite and anxious creatures, we can be so tempted to absolutise the present moment. As an eating-disordered person, I know this temptation all too well. When I am experiencing a carbohydrate craving, I become fearful that it will last forever; I begin to have panicky images of myself eating box after box of granola, day in and day out, with frantic hunger unabating. That very panic produces something of a self-fulfilling prophecy, a self-perpetuating binge which seeks to stuff down my anxious feelings. When I am surrounded by an abundance of foods that I love (in a setting like that of Susie Orbach's fantasy), I become frightened that they will not always be there, and so I feel an impulse at that moment to eat everything in sight as a hedge against future deprivation. The problem at the deep root of my bulimia (the problem at the deep root of our cultural food pathology) is an insufficiency of trust. I do not trust the rhythms of my own body to pass from times of craving to times of contentment. I do not trust the rhythms of life itself to move from times of abundance to times of austerity and back again.

The Christian calendar, with its punctuating feast days and fast days and "daily bread" days in between, attempts to teach us these rhythms. To learn from the calendar requires of us a third kind of spiritual practice, that of "attunement" or "fine-tuning" of the self. Margaret Miles's definition of spiritual practices highlights this dimension of attunement, speaking of the Christian life as a matter of "self-conscious, ongoing alertness to the need for correcting one's particular propensities." It is a spiritual discipline for me to tune in to my own body, to pay attention to its (her? our?) pains and pleasures, yearnings and satisfactions. It is a spiritual discipline for me to make myself eat slowly, savoring every mouthful, and stopping at the point when I sense my body has reached pleasurable satiation. It is a spiritual discipline for me to meditate a moment before meal preparation, attempting to discern exactly what it is I am wanting to eat—or even if I am wanting to eat at all. It is a spiritual discipline for me to learn when my body is signaling hunger (whether the clock says it is mealtime or not), and when my body is wanting something besides food (rest, recreation, touch, some other sensuous indulgence). In short, it is a spiritual discipline to "fine-tune" my awareness of myself as an embodied creature, to hear more acutely that inner corporeal wisdom that leads me in the direction of greater wholeness and health.

As Roberta Bondi notes in her historical study of patristic (and matristic) spiritual practices, "The assumption in the early literature is that it is the little things we do over a long period of time that form character and make our relationthips with ourselves, others, and God what they are."[47] The small choices we make every mealtime (and every between-meal time)—choices about appropriate pleasure seeking, appropriate abstaining, and appropriate sharing—develop our character for making choices in larger matters. Writing from a contemporary perspective, M. F. K. Fisher draws a similar conclusion: "The ability to choose what food [we] must eat, and knowingly, will make [us] able to choose other less transitory things with courage and finesse."[48] Fine-tuning our perceptions and our choices to heightened responsiveness and responsibility encourages us in shaping a spirituality of everyday life: a spirituality which brings together *Kirche* and *Küche*, sacred and secular, soul and body, in ways radically befitting a juicy and joyous theology of incarnation—a theology of the Word made flesh.

FOOD FOR THEOLOGICAL THOUGHT

I began this chapter a little over a month ago on a groggy morning, hung-over and self-hating from an eating binge of the night before. In drawing this chapter to a close, I note with some pleasure the synchronicity of the calendar. Today is Ash Wednesday, traditionally a fast day in the Christian year—a "morning after" day in its own right (and rite), following the indulgences of Shrove Tuesday, "Fat" Tuesday, *Mardi Gras*. Today marks the beginning of deliberate Lenten deprivations, intended to prepare our bodies and spirits for the glorious rejoicing of Easter. Fasting and feasting flow into one another, enrich one another in the "seasoning" of our lives.

Fasting and feasting, feeding the hungry, feeding ourselves fittingly, and sharing table fellowship with one another—these basic, earthy practices rest at the very foundations of Christian life and thought. As we ponder these practices, we can no longer help but conclude that our food-related behaviors are worthy of our attention. They are of broad scope, involving vast numbers of us in making immense investments of our money and attention and energy. They shape and are shaped by the orienting symbols and sacraments of our faith. They summon us to the task of developing a spirituality for the everydayness of our lives.

One anxious evening a little over a month ago, I systematically ate an entire ten-ounce box of granola. The next morning, I woke up hating myself. So what? So, finally, this: when I can, when *we* can at last stop our fearful and gnostic trivializing of such activities, we can come to appreciate that they offer us abundant food for theological thought. Such "thought food"—soul and body food—serves as an *apologia* and first course for the remainder of this book, which follows as a kind of movable feast. Our next course takes us into the halls of historical Christianity, as we continue our pilgrimage in metaphorical theology from the fruit trees of Eden toward the final banquet of the Lamb.

Gluttony—A Historical Digest

FORBIDDEN FRUIT

The fruit trees of Eden form the lush symbolic setting for the first human disobedience. The tale is familiar to our hearing. In the east, God planted a garden and caused to grow in it every tree that is pleasant to the sight and good for food. Then God molded a human creature out of the humus, enlivening it with God's own breath, and placed it in the garden to till and keep, serve and protect it. And God commanded the human one, saying:

> You may freely eat of every tree of the garden; but of the tree of the knowledge of good and evil you shall not eat, for in the day that you eat of it you shall die. (Gen. 2:16-17)

So the story begins—a story of stewardship and presumption, of transgression and healing; a story of pilgrimage from the forbidden fruit of Eden toward the final feast of redemption.

How are we to interpret this story? Even if we read it symbolically rather than literally, what are we to make of the fact that this foundational narrative of Judeo-Christian culture identifies the paradigmatic disobedience with an image of *eating*? While the story may intend to focus on the presumptuous transgression of a divine command and not on the specific act through which the transgression occurs, the detail remains that the violated prohibition involves a forbidden food. It could have been otherwise. God could have said: "In this cave, within this box, under this rock, beneath this tree are hidden the secrets of good and evil; you are not to loose them or to look upon them lest you die." The myths of other religions involve other images of primordial disobedience. The Judeo-Christian narrative involves eating. In a metaphorical theology oriented around images of food and feeding, such a fact should give us pause. Our very familiarity with the Eden story and its traditional interpretations may deafen our ears to this detail. Yet, the image of the "forbidden fruit" pervades our cultural mythology, in ways which may be as pernicious as the image of the woman as temptress, an allied legacy of the Genesis narrative.

The former image flavors, for example, our basic assumptions about pleasure: the forbidden fruit is always sweetest, we sigh, moving from that assumption to the corollary that if something is particularly pleasurable, it must be forbidden to us. How many times have we heard or uttered the lament: "Everything I like is either illegal, immoral, or fattening"? Indeed, in our modern-day myth-making, we come dangerously close to assuming an equation between the latter two adjectives. Our rhetoric of eating abounds with admonitions about "tempting" and "sinful" foods . . . as if what went into our bodies could ever defile them; as if we have forgotten what other foundational texts of the Christian faith teach on this very subject; as if we have forgotten that all the fruit trees of Eden but one were delightful to the eye and pleasing to the taste and also perfectly legitimate to enjoy.

In addition to flavoring our assumptions about pleasure, the "forbidden fruit" image also flavors (or sours) our conceptions of virtue. The person who abstains from eating takes on heroic qualities in our thinking; the modern-day dieter replaces the early Christian ascetic as one who is revered for great will power in resisting temptation. Anorexia nervosa, a disease of willful self-starvation, takes such heroics of self-control to life-threatening extremes. Yet, there are still those in our culture who secretly wish they could "catch" this disease in order to capitalize on its ability to resist forbidden fruits.

Our distrust of pleasure and our veneration of abstinence, even to the point of emaciation, confirm that our cultural values surrounding food and eating—as pleasure, vice, and virtue—are seriously skewed. We saw statistical documentation of this fact in the previous chapter. For the next two chapters, we will be exploring various sources from which these values arise. In particular, this chapter takes us into the documents of historical Christianity as we seek to discover what attitudes toward food such documents convey. Is the image of food as "forbidden fruit" a legitimate legacy of the Christian tradition—or is it, like the image of "woman as temptress," the result of fundamental distortions?

Of prime importance in our investigation will be materials which discuss the topic of eating by expounding upon the forbidden act, the "deadly sin" of *gluttony*. A number of questions will guide our study. What exactly is gluttony, in the traditional understandings of Christian theology? Why is it labeled sinful? Does this label mask the gnostic influences of an "other-worldly asceticism" (such as we discussed in the previous chapter); was it just monks and nuns in desert cells or cloistered retreats who were concerned to fight the demon of gluttony in order to kill the lusts of the flesh and draw closer to God? Or does the prohibition of gluttony also teach the average Christian man or woman in the world some fundamental wisdom about the ordering of bodily life? What is the relationship between gluttony as it is traditionally defined by the church and eating disorders as they pervade contemporary American culture? As we sample some vintage documents of Christian history in responding to these questions, we will come to an interesting discovery: that even though a few invitations to our currently skewed values emerge from our faith tradition, that tradition also contains some surprisingly helpful correctives to our distorted perspectives on food and the flesh.

SCRIPTURE

At a workshop on food and body image which I conducted not long ago at a conference devoted to women's issues in theology, a participant shared with me a letter she had received from the organization "Insight for Living," a group which claims itself to be "committed to excellence in communicating biblical truth and its application." In that letter appears the line, "the Word of God condemns . . . obesity."[1] The woman asked me if I, as a theologian, believed this statement to be true. In essence, she wanted to know whether or not the formative texts of Christian faith offer a theological warrant for the fat-phobia and dietary obsessiveness of modern western society.

The "Insight for Living" letter lists three supporting citations for its position on obesity: Romans 1:24-32, I Corinthians 5:11, and Galatians 5:19-21. I have read these texts with careful attention. In them, I see admonitions to avoid drunkenness and carousing (as well as idolatry, gossiping, and dissension), and directives to honor the body and practice self-control (as well as kindness, patience, and love). In the context surrounding them, I see distinctions being made between pursuing aims of the Spirit and gratifying desires of the *sarx* (which is often translated as "flesh," but which in Paul's lexicon means that which is selfish, willful, and God-defying, *not* that which is bodily). I find, however, no condemnation of obesity.

This is a crucial—and not a casuistic—consideration. It introduces a key theme which will be with us for the remainder of our study: a theme which asserts as stalwartly as it can that *girth* is not the same thing as *gluttony* (and vice versa). Where scripture speaks words of admonition and counsel, as it does in the passages noted above, it does so with regard to particular patterns of consumption, not to particular body shapes or sizes. Scripture is far more concerned with the measure of a person's total life than with the measure of her or his waistline: Does that life stretch out toward God or does it stay enclosed within the confines of self-will? In fact, to imply that the waist-measurement is what matters, such that in and of itself slenderness is more "godly" than obesity, is to come rather close to worshiping the form of the creature and not its Creator, the very idolatry which Romans 1 is most concerned to condemn. Forbidden fruits are not forbidden in the Bible because they are fattening; fat-phobia, indeed, marks a fairly *anti*-biblical preoccupation.

Gluttony, not girth, is the key issue for scripture. (If we took care of our gluttony, our girth might or might not take care of itself—a matter which we will examine further in the following chapters.) There are a few biblical texts which explicitly refer to gluttony: Proverbs 23, for example, and Chapter 31 of Ecclesiasticus (the Wisdom of Jesus, the Son of Sirach). Both these texts offer prudential counsel about seemliness in eating—for the purposes of avoiding poverty, social offensiveness, fitful sleep, or bad digestion. (Verse 21 of the apocryphal text even advises arising to vomit in the middle of a meal in order to have relief from overstuffing—probably not a verse which a spiritual director should offer a bulimic as a guide for meditation.) Deuteronomy 21:20 sternly ordains that a stubborn and rebellious son who is "a glutton and a drunkard" is to be stoned to death by the elders of his city.

Apart from these few direct references, however, the scriptural attitude toward food and eating is more to be found in indirection, in an overall "Symbolics and Sacramentality" of food, such as we sampled in the previous chapter. As Carl and LaVonne Braaten observe, "[Even though] the entire symbol system in the Bible and Christian faith is based on such natural functions as eating, drinking, and breathing . . . in the Bible we do not meet a metaphysics of food as in Oriental philosophy, with its theory about yin and yang."[2] Nor do we meet there a dogmatics of diet: unlike Judaism, Islam, Hinduism, and Buddhism, Christianity states no laws of kosher, proscribes no specific foods, prescribes no specific abstinence.[3] Rather, what we meet in Christian scripture is a remarkable balance in attitudes toward eating. Put briefly, this balance affirms that food is good—but is not a supreme good; and that care taken with food is important—but not of paramount importance.

Food is good. Jesus himself is labeled "a glutton and a drunkard" (and meets with clear disapproval from the elders of various cities).[4] While the Pharisees and the disciples of John the Baptist fast, the disciples of Jesus eat and drink to celebrate the presence of the "bridegroom," their Beloved. Jesus tells parables likening the realm of God to a great banquet or a marriage feast. At an actual wedding in Cana, Jesus changes water into wine as the first "sign" of his God-fullness. Jesus dines with tax collectors and sinners; he teaches his followers to pray that they may receive their daily bread; he miraculously feeds four thousand, five thousand people. He eats one final Passover meal with his dearest friends, choosing bread and wine to be the lasting sacrament of his coming death and of his abiding presence. After the resurrection, he makes himself known in the grilling of fish and the breaking of bread. Simple gestures of feeding testify to the graciousness of God—and to the grace-fullness of food.

Food itself is good—but food is not a supreme good. We are to pray for our daily bread, but we must also know that we do not live by bread alone.[5] "Is not life more than food? " Jesus gently admonishes us. Trust in God should cast out our anxiety about what we shall have to eat or to drink. As testimony to our trust in God's providence, and as attunement of ourselves to that which *is* supremely important, fasting can be an appropriate discipline. Jesus himself fasts for forty days in the wilderness in preparation for his ministry. Just as the gospels overflow in a celebration of God's grace, they also abound in exhortations to self-giving and self-denial. The rich man who feasts while Lazarus starves at the gate serves as the very prototype of wickedness. Feeding the poor is a hallmark of discipleship. Woe be unto those who are full now, for they (or we?) shall ultimately hunger. Blessed are those who hunger, for they shall be satisfied.

Because food is not itself a supreme good, it is fitting to exercise care and restraint with regard to eating. Just as Jesus fasts in the wilderness, so he also expects the disciples to fast once the bridegroom has departed from their midst. Indeed, the book of Acts notes that the earliest Christians worship with fasting and with prayer.[6] The Pauline letters and the Pastoral epistles make numerous references to physical restraint, warning against greed and drunkenness and counseling temperance and self-control (but never expressly condemning obesity). While not explicitly mentioning food, the second letter of Timothy strongly condemns those who are "lovers of pleasure rather than lovers of God" (but says nothing about those who are lovers of pleasure *because* they are lovers of a beauty- and pleasure-creating God).

In perhaps the strongest text against gluttony in Christian Scripture, Paul predicts an end in destruction for those "[whose] god is the belly." We are to exercise care that the pleasures of eating do not distract us from more lastingly important matters; we are not to make an idol out of any form of merely physical gratification.

But by the same token, we are not to make into an idol any particular form of spiritual practice. Care about what and how we feed ourselves is important—but it is not of paramount importance. The early Jesus community experiences freedom from specific dietary restrictions. Jesus himself declares all foods clean, insisting that the real danger of defilement lies in evil thoughts and actions which come out of our hearts, and not in unclean foods which enter our stomachs.[7] (I confess I find myself wondering what relevance this distinction might have to differentiating between the gravity of "obesity" itself and the gravity of judgmental remarks about obesity as evidence of sin.) Paul carries forward Jesus' teaching. While Christians are to be careful that their newfound freedom not be taken as an invitation to license by those who might be "weaker" than they, nonetheless followers of the Christ are not bound to any ceremonial laws with regard to eating. "Food will not commend us to God," Paul writes; "We are no worse off if we do not eat, and no better off if we do." Or in another balanced pronouncement with wide-ranging implications: "Let not the one who eats despise the one who abstains, and let not the one who abstains pass judgment on the one who eats." In warning against false teachers who put on an appearance of wisdom in their exhortations of "severity to the body," Paul notes that such severities are in fact "of no value in checking the indulgence of the flesh"—a note which makes it abundantly clear that "flesh" and "body" are not synonymous in his thinking. The First Letter to Timothy gives further clarity to the distinction between false teachings of bodily severity and true teachings of Christian freedom. In strong language, this Pastoral epistle cautions against "liars" who "enjoin abstinence from foods which God created to be received with thanksgiving. . . . For everything created by God is good." Food itself is a part of God's creation which is to be enjoyed. What will commend us to God is not feats of dietary righteousness, but rather the festivity of thankful receiving.

Christian scripture thus provides the basis for a healthily balanced theology of eating. Taken in the totality of its teachings, the Bible focuses neither on "forbidden fruits" nor on offensive fatness, but rather on perfidious attitudes. *Food* itself is good. *Girth* in and of itself is not an issue. But *gluttony* does represent a problem for both testaments insofar as it endangers physical health and social well-being. Even more seriously, gluttony is labeled a sin insofar as it focuses on the willful pursuit of personal pleasure to the exclusion of any greater value—including that of gratitude to the Supreme Source of all good pleasure, namely God.

PATRISTIC AND MONASTIC WRITINGS

In the first few centuries after the recording of scripture, this balanced perspective loses some of its equilibrium. The writings of the Church Fathers ("patristic" texts) begin to display a greater ambivalence about eating than might seem warranted by the life of Jesus or the teachings of Paul and the Pastoral epistles. This ambivalence can be traced to a number of contributing factors. One is simply a reaction against the excesses of contemporary culture. M. F. K. Fisher vividly describes the debauchery to which Rome sinks in the days of its decay:

> Satiety, that monster behind pleasure, breathed into the stuffed bellies of the Romans. Excitants to their palates were prerequisites—those palates by now so ill-treated that some of the gourmets were forced to wear little tongue gloves to protect their delicate taste-glands from all but the most exotic flavors. . . . Emetics were served with the beginning courses of any longer dinner. . . . *Vomitoria* came into being.[8]

It is little wonder that, confronted with such a ghastly spectacle, early Christian writers intensify their cautions against the possibilities of gluttonous excess.

A second significant factor in intensifying Christian ambivalence toward eating lies in the emergence of the monastic movement. Seeing clearly the dangers of life in a decadent society, and lacking the outlet of martyrdom which allowed earlier Christians to follow in the self-sacrificing footsteps of their Lord, men and women of the fourth century begin seeking other paths of self-denial. Flight to the desert to do lonely battle with the demons of worldliness and self-will becomes one such path. Indeed, it grows to be so popular that the initially lonely or "eremetic" retreat enlarges to become communal or "cenobitic" life in devotion to God rather than to self or to the dictates of society. The tradition of the "seven deadly sins" emerges out of this monastic movement, first in the writings of Evagrius Ponticus and subsequently in the work of his student, John Cassian.[9] The man or woman intent on complete submission to God attempts to vanquish all desires which threaten to distract him or her from that end. Primacy of place in the deadly sin tradition is given to the "demon" or "passion" of gluttony. Conquest of the appetite for food constitutes the first stage in a monastic battle campaign which enjoins rigorous physical and spiritual self-discipline. An "other-worldly asceticism" attempts to annihilate the pleasures of earth in pursuit of the far sweeter rewards of heaven.

A third factor which intensifies ambivalence toward the earthiness of eating in patristic and monastic writings emerges from the influences of contemporary philosophical movements. Herbert Musurillo meticulously diagnoses strains of Cynic, Stoic, and Neoplatonic thought in what he calls the "anti-matter asceticism" of many Christian authors in the Hellenistic world.[10] Where the former two movements teach a general ethical suspicion of pleasure and promotion of *apatheia* or dispassionate equanimity, the last-mentioned of the three holds to a metaphysical dualism between superior, potentially free-soaring spirit and inferior, imprisoning flesh. When Christianity spreads to the Gentile world, it adapts to these Greek Hellenistic modes of thinking which increasingly divert it from the Hebraic earthiness of its origins—origins in a rabbi who enjoins no extraordinary food asceticism, who eats and drinks with friends and enemies, who lives a fully incarnate existence as the Word *made flesh*. In fact, so far removed from these roots does some early patristic writing become that Clement of Alexandria contends Jesus did not eat or drink from bodily need but only because he wanted to convince the disciples of his humanness; and Basil of Caesarea makes the astounding claim that when Jesus ate, "He did not even pass His food, so great was the power of self-control in Him."[11]

These three factors of opposition to Roman decadence, pursuit of monastic holiness, and permeation by Hellenistic philosophy combine to make patristic exhortations against the pleasures of food far more stringent than earlier scriptural teaching. Evagrius Ponticus is not alone in his insistence that gluttony is the first sin of Adam and Eve as well as the first deadly sin against which the aspiring monk must do battle. Abbot Nilus, a monastic spiritual director of the fifth century, asserts in his tract on the "eight spirits of evil" that "the desire of food . . . spawned disobedience" and that "it was the pleasure of taste that drove us from Paradise." Gregory of Nyssa in his treatise on virginity maintains that the pleasure of taste is "mother of all vice."[12] These three authors clearly recall what many more "modern" thinkers among us appear to have forgotten: that the original transgression among the fruit trees of Eden involved an act of *eating*.

The flesh-spirit dualism of Neoplatonic thinking becomes particularly apparent in some forms of patristic condemnation of gluttony. Not only is dietary indulgence seen (as in scripture) to represent a willful pursuit of personal pleasures in defiance of the will of God. Food is further seen as a literal "weight" or drag on the human spirit. Several authors seem to conflate corpulence with corporeality (or bodily, as *opposed* to spiritual, life). While the Bible itself says nothing about slenderness as a virtue or obesity as a sin, various monastic writers come much closer to this position. Abbot Daniel insists: "As the body waxes fat, the soul grows thin; and as the body grows thin, the soul by so much waxes fat." Saint Jerome teaches that "the attenuation, the slenderness, the deliverance of the body from the encumbrance of much flesh, gives us . . . some conformity to God and His angels." Basil claims that "leanness of body . . . [marks] the Christian," and sounds particularly Neoplatonic (if not gnostic) in his admonition:

> Recall Pythagoras who, whenever he saw one of his pupils getting too fat because of lack of proper diet and exercise, used to say: Why don't you stop making your prison more difficult for you?[13]

Chrysostom reveals similar Neoplatonist leanings in his threats that food will "bury the soul alive and make the wall about it all the thicker." Indeed, it is Chrysostom who pens the most graphic (and fat-phobic) denunciation of gluttony in all patristic literature when he describes the "disgusting spectacle of the obese man, dragging his body along like a seal" and the debauchee arising on the morning after a binge, "like a fat pig, his eyes rheumy . . . dragging his great weight of flesh around like an elephant."[14]

Yet, on the other hand, even with this harsh condemnation of fatness, the writings of Chrysostom against gluttony and drunkenness also disclose another attitude—an attitude which reveals that the biblical equilibrium in attitudes toward eating has not been wholly unbalanced by the Neoplatonism of patristic and monastic asceticism. In a wonderfully creation-affirming passage, Chrysostom exhorts: "Enjoy your baths, your good table, your meat, your wine in moderation—enjoy everything in fact, but keep away from sin!" The wisdom of the scriptural position appears here in a hearty affirmation that all God's creations are good, if received with the proper attitude. Sin lies in a *manner* of consumption, not in consumption itself. In his commentary on Matthew, Origen reiterates this insight. Food is never unclean in and of itself, but only when obtained out of avarice or consumed by an appetite which is allowed to overrule our reason. Neither food nor bodily hunger is to blame for the sinfulness of gluttony. As Gregory of Nyssa maintains: "The body merely gives a sign that there is need of nourishment; it is [human] will that perverts [this] need."[15] Willfulness, not bodiliness, is the root of sin.

The biblical equilibrium also reappears in some teachings of the patristic and monastic authors with regard to fasting. While there do exist gnostic and Neoplatonic extremes of bodily mortification, the countering Christian attitude insists on moderation. Origen notes, in harmony with the teachings of Jesus, that there is a sense in which the Christian cannot properly fast, because "Christ, the Bridegroom, though in heaven, is still with us." What we can do as a spiritual discipline instead, he suggests, is to engage in a fast from sin, and to feed the poor. As other Christian writers preach from the patristic era through the Middle Ages, any physical fast is to be supplemented by the more important act of giving food away to those in need.[16]

In addition to tempering fasting with charity and with celebration of the presence of the Beloved, patristic authors also note how austerity is always to be modified by hospitality. Stories of the desert fathers and mothers abound in illustrations of their equilibrated gentility. One such story tells of a group of visitors from Palestine who arrive at the dwelling of an Egyptian hermit. Immediately the man arises from his prayers in order to prepare a meal for his guests. They eat his food and then dare to criticize him for what they take to be his lack of austerity. The host monk gently replies:

> Fasting is ever with me, but I cannot keep you ever here.... Receiving Christ in you, I must show you whatever things be of love, with all carefulness: but when I have sent you away, then may I take up again the rule of fasting.[17]

Even when not mitigated by the greater law of love, the rule of fasting is to be observed only in moderation. Extreme feats of austerity are seen to issue from demonic rather than divine commandments. St. Syncletice, a fourth-century desert teacher, proclaims:

> The devil sometimes sends a severe fast, too prolonged.... How do we distinguish the fasting of our God . . . from the fasting of that tyrant the devil? Clearly by its moderation.... Everything which is extreme is destructive.[18]

Evagrius similarly notes in his writings on the deadly sins that demons encourage the weak to attempt "feats of fasting." Cassian is clear that one possible outcome of underindulgence is a backlash of overindulgence: "Austere fasts which give rise to an exaggerated relaxation of discipline," he writes, "are good for nothing and soon lead to gluttony." Instead of such extremes, he counsels that "a reasonable and moderate meal each day" is better than "an austere fast prolonged over several days." Thus, the ascetic can avoid any "lassitude" or loss of vigor in prayer.[19]

Extremes of underindulgence are thus looked upon as severely by many patristic authors as are extremes of overindulgence. Christian monasticism as a whole—particularly in the

Benedictine Rule—invokes a norm that affirms both restraint and moderation. As excessive fasting is carefully differentiated from appropriate discipline, so gluttony is carefully differentiated from eating itself, which is both necessary and good. The defining marks of gluttonous behavior are variously identified by different authors. Evagrius warns against seeking unnecessary *variety* in food, such that one forgets to be grateful and satisfied with "a mere morsel of bread." Basil speaks sternly about the perils of "nibbling in secret" and lying about one's eating, even to the point of stealing food and consuming it on the sly. Cassian labels three forms of gluttony as eating before the communally designated hour for meals, gorging oneself without regard to the quality of the food which one is eating, and seeking out particularly delicate or luxurious foods.[20] In all these instances, it is clear that the labeling of gluttony as a sin has little to do with a negative mythology of "forbidden fruits" or of forbidden fatness. Rather, it has to do with a life-affirming code of conduct which stresses simplicity, gratitude, openness, community spirit, care for the fruits of creation, and self-control.

Admittedly, the patristic and monastic attitude toward eating shows itself to be dated in certain ways. Evagrius' caution against variety, for example, draws upon a Hippocratic notion—widely accepted in the early Christian centuries—that all foods contain the same basic "universal aliment," such that eating a diversified diet would seem to serve only a decorative, and not a fundamentally nutritional, end.[21] Neoplatonic suspicions of bodily pleasures, and even of bodily shape and size, do at times appear. The "demon" of gluttony is the first one to be engaged in monastic battle during an era of scarcity in which thoughts of food may prove all the more distracting because the reality of the next meal is so unsure. In an era which encourages sexual abstinence, gluttonous indulgence of the appetite for food becomes even more threatening because a full stomach is thought to exert pressure on the sexual organs and thus to fan the flames of lust.[22] The philosophy and physiology of the fourth and fifth centuries belong to a clearly different world from the modern day. And yet. . . .

And yet there is still much we can learn from attending to the teachings of fourth- and fifth-century theologians and spiritual directors. Just as scripture teaches us a balanced attitude toward food and eating, so monastic and patristic authors help us discover a certain wisdom about the proper ordering of bodily life. Even given occasional tendencies toward a gnostic or "otherworldly" asceticism, overall their writings stress a "this-worldly" ethic, celebrating the previously-named values of simplicity, gratitude, honesty, community spirit, care for the fruits of creation, and self-control. Insofar as our eating is in accord with these values, it is healthful in both bodily and spiritual ways; insofar as it departs from them, it becomes destructive. Ultimately, such values offer a better way to measure the "fittingness" of our food lives than any calorie counter or tape measure or bathroom scale could ever provide.

PASTORAL CARE: GREGORY THE GREAT

Even if the fourth- and fifth-century writings on gluttony which we have just examined articulate a number of generally useful principles for the ordering of bodily life, those writings are still primarily intended for a monastic audience. By the sixth century, a new genre of theological literature is emerging to address the needs of lay people for spiritual discipline and direction. Gregory the Great's ground-breaking manual for pastoral care is a prime example of this literature. It provides a fascinating window into the daily spiritual concerns and practices of an earlier Christian era, and at the same time offers helpful historical perspective on the spiritual (or often less than spiritual) preoccupations of the present day.

The man who is known to Christian history as "Gregory the Great" reluctantly assumes the duties of the papacy in the year 590. He has no aspirations to administrative power; he would prefer to remain a simple Benedictine monk. He takes the reins of office because he feels responsive to the needs of an empire and a church in crisis: from attacks on Roman citizens by Lombard invaders; from the ravages of the plague; from general administrative disarray. Gregory's importance in the growth of temporal power for the papacy is enormous. So is his impact on Christian missions to the British Isles, and his influence on liturgical reforms within the Western church (hence, the naming of "Gregorian" chant in his honor). But through all his administrative efficiency and initiative, Gregory retains the heart of a pastor: one who is foremost concerned to lead his ever-widening flock in the paths of righteousness.

It is as a pastor that Gregory writes his most famous work, the *Liber Regulae Pastoralis*, otherwise known as the *Pastoral Care*. In it, he transposes the "deadly sins" tradition from a monastic into a more popular, devotional context. He writes of how a "ruler" is to teach and admonish those who are under his care, and takes pains to note that different admonishments are needed for people in different conditions of life: men and women, poor and rich, joyful and sad, dull and wise, humble and haughty. One of his pairings in particular has pertinence to a theological study of eating behaviors: the pairing of the gluttonous and the abstemious.

Gregory addresses this pairing in Admonition 20 of the *Pastoral Care*.[23] "Those who are addicted to gluttony are to be admonished in one way," he writes; "those who are abstemious in another (147)." What was implicit in many of the monastic writings here becomes explicit: it is just as inappropriate for Christian practice to be overly scrupulous with food as to be overly self-indulgent. Even as gluttony gives rise to other "sins of the tongue" such as loquacity and undue levity, so excessive abstinence is all too likely to issue in the correlated evils of pride and impatience. Gregory quotes approvingly the balanced Pauline injunction: "He that eateth not, let him not judge him that eateth (148)." With rare pastoral and psychological acuity, he adds:

> The abstemious are to be admonished to be always carefully on their guard that in fleeing from the vice of gluttony, worse vices are not generated, as it were, of virtue; that in mortifying the flesh, they do not break out in impatience of the spirit. There is no virtue in subduing the flesh, if the spirit is overcome by anger (149).

Nor is there any virtue in subduing the flesh if the spirit is overcome by self-righteous pride in this very accomplishment! Not only can excessive fasting provide a spur to pride and to angry or self-righteous judgments against one's fellows. It can also prove destructive of one's own body. Gregory comments that there are dangers afoot "when the flesh is worn by abstinence more than is necessary" (148–9). Extrapolating from this point, Robert Gillet notes in his introduction to another of Gregory's key ethical treatises (*Morals on the Book of Job*): "Il faut garder la tempérance de façon à tuer non la chair, mais les vices de la chair."[24] We must maintain temperance in order to kill not the flesh itself, but the vices of the flesh.

Like his patristic predecessors, Gregory agrees that one of the most important exercises in overcoming the vices of the flesh is the practice of charity. Ultimately, giving food to the poor is of far greater importance as a spiritual discipline than denying food to oneself (150). The fast which God chooses is a fast of giving bread to those who hunger. "How little the virtue of abstinence is regarded," Gregory remarks, "unless it deserve commendation by reason of other virtues" (150). Refraining from eating, in and of itself, avails nothing—and may even weaken our bodies or tempt our spirits to intolerance. Taking care with what we feed ourselves commends us to God only when we demonstrate at least equivalent care for the feeding of others.

With his critique of abstemiousness, Gregory surely figures among the moralists whom medievalist Bridget Ann Henisch has in mind when she concludes:

> Rigorous diets when endured merely for the sake of health received as little sympathy from sharp-eyed commentators on gluttony as ostentatious dinner parties. Dieting for fashion had not yet been invented, but we may be sure that moralists would have risen with relish to the challenge.[25]

Indeed. Gregory himself is keen on charting a middle course between overly scrupulous denial and ostentatious indulgence. In the admonitions of his *Pastoral Care*, he clearly insists that neither underindulgence nor overindulgence represents fitting Christian behavior.

In his *Morals on Job*, Gregory further discusses the dangers of the latter extreme. Fond of systematizing, he takes Cassian's comments on the deadly sin of gluttony and expands them to identify five (rather than Cassian's three) types of gluttonous behavior—namely, eating *praepropere* (too soon), *laute* (too expensively), *nimis* (too much), *ardenter* (too eagerly), or *studiose* (with too much attention).[26] It is interesting to note in this schema that Gregory gives only partial attention to the phenomenon of eating *too much*—the act which we tend in modern thinking to associate primarily (if not exclusively) with gluttony. We might do well to reflect further on his other four categories.

In fact, when I read Gregory, I find myself drawn into such reflection, as if in conversation with a good pastoral counselor. I find myself beginning to understand a little better why it is appropriate to look at some of my (our, our culture's) eating behaviors under the rubric of "sin." We may no longer observe the canonical hours as did Cassian and Gregory, or the medieval tradition that the first and main meal of the day is to be eaten at *none* (the ninth hour after daybreak—the origin of our word "noon"), only after morning devotionals and many hours of dutiful labor. But I suspect many of us who are compulsive eaters and dieters can sympathize with the poor sinner, depicted in the medieval *Book of Vices and Virtues*, whose first prayer of the morning is the plaintive cry: "A, lord God, what schule we ete today?"[27] I remember Ellen West, I remember myself, awaking daily to the consuming dread of eating and of not eating alike. And so Gregory's condemnation of the first form of gluttony as eating *praepropere*—too soon—begins to make sense. Something is being suggested here about the proper orientation of priorities. Am I, are we so consumed by anticipation of eating—or by dread of losing control over our eating—that we forget to begin each day in gratitude: for the gift of a new day at all, regardless of how we may proceed to feed ourselves within it?

Likewise for eating *ardenter*, too eagerly, and *studiose*, with too much attention: both these forms of gluttony also involve the misorientation of our priorities. The difference between eating eagerly and eating *too* eagerly calls to mind the distinction between feasting and bingeing, made in the previous chapter. Feasting turns with delight to the gifts of God's creation in order to savor and enjoy them. Bingeing, on the other hand, focuses so intently on the voracious act of consumption that particular tastes and textures no longer even matter. Bingeing does not savor; it devours. This point is even made through etymology: the root meaning of gluttony (*gula* in the Latin) anchors in the word for *gullet*, not for palate.

Eating *studiose*, with too much studied attention, lies at the opposite extreme from eating so eagerly that no attention at all is paid to what is being eaten. The person who eats *studiose* is extraordinarily fastidious about matters of diet. Those of us who count calories obsessively (or anyone who has ever tried to dine with someone who does) can readily relate to this form of gluttony, though it may seem odd to give it such a name. In a culture which facilely identifies the sin of gluttony as eating too much and the wages of this sin as being "too fat," it comes as a shock to recognize that Gregory's pastoral insights also locate gluttonous possibilities in eating too little and parading about in a shape of slender "perfection." The issue, to repeat, is one of priorities. If I have made the food I eat or the body I indwell into a focus for my relentless attention, I have created an idol, have elevated a part of the creation to the role which only the Creator should occupy. The price of such idolatry is the malaise which many among us are experiencing: the loss of any sustaining sense of personal worth or earthly delight apart from the superficial contingencies of appearance and utility; the loss of any ability to affirm that I am, that we are, that the fruits of the earth are good simply by virtue of being God's creations, regardless of presumed physical attractiveness or caloric value.

Eating too early, too eagerly, or with too much attention all reveal problems in the orientation of our priorities. So, obviously, does eating *laute*, too expensively: when feeding the hungry is the hallmark of discipleship, spending disproportionate sums to feed myself is clearly a breach of loyalties. Nor need the act of eating too expensively necessarily entail the quantity or sumptuousness of food consumed. I imagine, were Gregory transplanted into the present day, his pastoral and ethical exhortations would have a few choice things to say about the amount of money we pour into the diet industry. When children around the world and in our own communities still go to bed hungry every night, the fact that Americans spend $11.4 billion annually on low calorie soft drinks indicates something significant about the "gluttonous" misalign-ment of our values.[28]

So gluttony, for Gregory, has to do with an undervaluing of God, of the fruits of the earth, and of our neighbors. Surprisingly, perhaps, it has little if anything to do with the shape of our bodies (except insofar as we eat too fastidiously in pursuit of a particular bodily configuration). What was true for scripture is also true for Gregory's sixth-century pastoral counseling: *gluttony is not the same thing as girth*. In fact, the equation of the two phenomena hints at a peculiarly modern and neo-gnostic phenomenon. As Roy Porter reminds us, the fat-phobic perspective of the twentieth century did not obtain throughout the middle ages. *Then*, as opposed to now:

> The man able to stand feasts or run soup kitchens for the poor was recognized to be the grand man. The fat man was . . . the visible embodiment of the successful man . . . This prevalent symbolism of body size and shape is, of course, utterly alien in the light of the fashionable connotations of today's Western societies of super-abundance, where fat is corrupt—diseased even—and lean is fit.[29]

Alien though it may be, this conception does show us that our modern equations of fat with evil and lean with good are at best historically relative, and at worst, dangerously skewed.

PENITENTIAL HANDBOOKS

In addition to the pastoral and ethical treatises of Gregory the Great, the penitential literature of the sixth through twelfth centuries provides an intriguing historical contrast of past food-related concerns with present dietary preoccupations. Of princi-pally Celtic origin, penitential handbooks emerge in Ireland in the late sixth century, spread into England, and thence, through the work of Anglo-Saxon missionary monks, into the Frankish territories of Western Europe. These handbooks provide guide-lines for the newly developing practice of private penance, replac-ing once-in-a-lifetime confession before the entire church with regular confession before an individual spiritual director in order to receive appropriate acts of expiation to perform.[30] Tailoring penances to age, rank, sex, clerical status, and gravity of offense, the confessors' manuals attempt to confer a degree of uniformity and order upon Christian practice in a seemingly chaotic world.

In general, the penitential handbooks follow either Cassian's or Gregory's orderings of the deadly sins, giving a significant place to the evil of gluttony. Fasting on bread and water is the customary penance assigned to gluttonous acts, on the generally accepted principle, clearly stated in the seventh-century Irish Penitential of Cummean: "Contraries are cured by contraries, [and the one] who freely commits what is forbidden ought freely to restrain himself [or herself] from what is otherwise permissible."[31] Occasionally, gluttony is identified in ways familiar from earlier discussions: eating before the canonical hour for meals, taking more delicate food than is available to others, or consuming too great a quantity of food or drink, which is now graphically depicted as filling oneself to the point of "distention of the stomach," or even "to the point of vomiting (101)." In other instances, however, new shades of intriguing local color become visible in the medieval handbooks.

One such shade can best be understood as depicting a tacit concern for hygiene. How else can we interpret such seemingly bizarre prescriptions as are found in the early ninth-century *Old Irish Penitential*? For example:

> 2. Anyone who ... drinks the blood or urine of an animal, does penance for three years and a half.

> 3. Anyone who eats flesh which dogs or beasts have been eating, or who eats carrion, or drinks the liquid in which the carrion is ... does penance for forty nights on bread and water.

> 4. Anyone who drinks liquid in which there is a dead mouse does seven days' penance therefor (157).

These rules and penances clearly apply to a different historical era from our own—an era of either such strong stomachs or such scarce food and drink that the church would have to warn people sternly away from eating carrion or the liquid in which it has been lying!

These hygienic considerations come as close as any documents within Christian history to establishing a distinction between kosher and non-kosher, clean and unclean foods.[32] While such laws themselves may have little applicability to the present, the fact that medieval prohibitions against gluttony contain such tacit concerns for sanitation and health offers a note-worthy precedent for modern food- and health-related interests in Christian theology and ethics. Further proscriptions from the penitentials are even more difficult to translate out of their historically colorful context: for example, the *Roman Penitential of Halitgar* (C.E. 830) mentions penances designed to counter lingering loyalties to indigenous religions by condemning the "gluttonous" act of eating at a "pagan" sacred site (306).

Even with the vivid local color of the penitential literature, it continues for the most part in the scriptural, patristic, and Gregorian tradition of offering a prudent balance of counsel regarding eating and not eating. If excessive eating is condemned, so too is excessive fasting. The *Old Irish Penitential* prescribes a week's penance for the sacrilege of fasting, "through carelessness or austerity," on a Sunday (159). On the even greater feast days of the church, such as Easter and Christmas, anyone who has taken a vow not to partake of flesh, bacon, butter, beer, or milk must abandon austerity in order "to take three morsels or three sips of each of them (158)." Vows of abstinence are also to be relaxed in order to accept hospitality. In a truly remarkable passage on the relaxations of discipline permissible in times of feasting, this ninth-century penitential concludes:

> Anyone who eats food or drinks beer until he vomits . . . does thirty days' penance. . . . [But] if this . . . happens . . . in rejoicings at the eight festivals of the year, or if it be a confessor's repast, or if it be on holy feast days . . . in all such cases *there is no harm* (159, my emphasis).

The eleventh-century *Confessor of Burchard of Worms* carries forward the prohibitions against fasting on feast days, and adds (with Pauline and Gregorian resonance): "Hast thou despised anyone who when thou was fasting could not fast and was eating? If thou hast, thou shalt do penance for five days on bread and water (332)." In short, for the medieval penitential handbooks, there are far more serious transgressions than those which involve overeating: for example, those transgressions of "over-fasting" which undermine tolerance and depress true festivity and thanksgiving.

SCHOLASTIC SUMMATION

For all of their merits in attempting to order Christian life through the so-called "Dark Ages" into a hygienic and well-balanced regimen of indulgence and self-discipline, the medieval penitential handbooks nevertheless possess the drawback of being occasionally disorderly among themselves. The penances they suggest for similar infractions can vary widely. In the mid-eleventh century, theologian Peter Damian attacks the whole genre of confessors' handbooks as being without sufficient authority.[33] At best, for him or for us, what this literature offers is a diverse, instructive, and historically colorful compendium of possible misdeeds and appropriate remedies, loosely grouped around the framework of the deadly sins tradition. At worst, it supplies a rather scattershot approach to the "cure of souls," and may even suggest a greater variety of temptations to the confessing sinner than he or she might otherwise imagine!

To move from scattershot to more systematic approaches, we must turn (as Peter Damian begins to do) from the popular writings of the pastoral and penitential traditions to the more specialized disquisitions of the theological "schoolmen" or scholastics. Chief among them is the Dominican scholar, Thomas Aquinas, whose *Summa Theologiae* constitutes an impressive summation and systematization of every question of "faith and morals" conceivable to a thirteenth-century thinker.

Thomas himself presents an appealing case study for a historical theology of eating. His own girth reaches legendary proportions. Huge and lumbering, he acquires the nickname "The Dumb Ox" by those who ignorantly mistake his ponderousness for stupidity.[34] Stories report that a special semicircular opening had to be cut in his desk so that he could bring his body close enough to the writing surface to be able to work. Other stories imply that at mealtimes he would get so engrossed in thought that he would forget he was eating and just keep unwittingly consuming more and more. Yet, for all his girth, no one would ever think to deride Thomas Aquinas as a glutton. In fact, he could in good conscience write an entire section on the vice of gluttony in his theological *Summa*. It is to that section which we turn in search of systematic clarity on the distinctions between the evils of gluttony the innocence of simple eating.

Before opening the pages of the *Summa*, however, it is useful to note two further contextual factors which influence Thomas' perspective on eating. First among them is the fact that Dominican theology has its origins in a battle against dualistic heresy—particularly, the heresy of the Albigensians who decry all matter, including the human body, as fundamentally evil. In opposition to such neo-gnosticism, Thomas insists that the body itself is good, having been created by God and further sanctified by the miracle of incarnation. The second contextual factor has to do with the tools which Thomas employs in his battle against dualism: namely, the tools of Aristotelian, rather than Platonic, philosophy. Platonism tends to promote a dualistic rejection of the body and the earth, as we saw in the "anti-matter asceticism" of Greek patristic authors under the influence of Neoplatonic thought. Aristotelianism, on the other hand, promotes a holistic appreciation of the body and of matter as the very *realities* in and through which truth comes to be.

Thomas Aquinas, therefore, is an Aristotelian realist, an anti-Albigensian apologist, and a radically incarnational theologian. As such, he asserts—against a long stream of ascetic austerity—that bodily pleasure, within reason, is *good*.[35] Indeed, he goes so far as to insist:

> Nature has introduced pleasure into the operations that are necessary for human life. Wherefore the natural order requires that a human being should make use of these pleasures, insofar as they are necessary . . . as regards the preservation either of the individual [through eating] or of the species [through sex]. Accordingly, if anyone were to reject pleasure to the extent of omitting things

that are necessary for nature's preservation, that person would sin. (IIaIIae, 142, 1)

To reject the pleasures of food, given to us for the preservation of our bodies, is to commit one of the two types of sins opposing temperance: the sin of "insensibility."

To overdo the pleasures of food, however, is to commit the correlated sin of gluttony. In articulating his definition of this particular form of intemperance, Thomas takes pains to clarify what gluttony is *not*. The sinfulness of gluttony does not inhere in the substance of food itself, which is good (in contrast to the claims of the "Manicheans"—a dualistic, gnostic sect—who pronounce certain foods literally unclean). Nor does sin lie in the physical appetites of hunger and thirst, which themselves are "neither virtue nor vice." Finally, overeating is not sinful when it proceeds from ignorance or inexperience—from thinking, for example, that large quantities of food are necessary for survival (or, presumably, from forgetting that one is eating when lost in celestial contemplation!) (IIaIIae, 148, 1).

What defines gluttony as a sin is the fact that it knowingly "departs from the reasonable order of life" and gives way to inordinate and unrestrained desire. Thomas quotes with approval Gregory's five categories of gluttony (eating too early, too expensively, too much, too eagerly, and with too much attention). "Inordinateness," he says, may affect either food itself or the act of eating:

> As for the stuff itself, we may want it sumptuous and costly; as for the quality, we may want it overdressed [*accurate praeparatos*]; and as for quantity, we may take overmuch. Then as for eating, we may anticipate the proper time or . . . [we may eat] feverishly. (IIaIIae, 148, 4)

The gravity of gluttony is "mitigated" both "because of our need to take food and because of the difficulty of applying proper discretion and moderation in the matter (IIaIIae, 148, 3)." However, the practice of gluttony can become mortally sinful when a preoccupation with eating displaces love for God and overrides any other purpose in living (IIaIIae, 148, 2). In any case, "our guilt is increased by the bodily damage we do to ourselves by our immoderate eating (IIaIIae, 148, 3)." Thus, for example, while "vomiting is good when we have eaten overmuch, yet it is sinful to subject ourselves to the necessity by lack of moderation" (IIaIIae, 148, 6).

"Lack of moderation" is, indeed, the key phrase which sounds throughout Thomas' writings on sinful eating behaviors. The phrase applies not only to excesses in indulgence, but also to excesses in austerity. Just as "insensibility" is a sin opposing temperance by failing to appreciate the pleasures given to us to adorn our most basic needs for individual and species preservation, so even fasting can become a sin against temperance when it is "not in accord with right reason." Immoderate abstinence can eat away at both patience and humility, as Gregory the Great has already observed. The rule which we should follow in fasting is as follows:

> namely that in abstaining from food we should act with due regard for those among whom we live, for our own person, and for the requirements of health.

Once we have appropriately attended to our neighbors and our bodies, we should finally make sure when we deny ourselves the pleasures of food that we are doing so "for the due end, i.e. for God's glory, and not our own (IIaIIae, 146, 1)."

If we are looking for guidelines to help regulate our food lives—guidelines that take into account the deep theological significance of the ways in which we feed or abstain from feeding ourselves—Thomas Aquinas' thirteenth-century treatment of temperance and intemperance offers us an enormously helpful systematization and summation of key issues. First, he re-affirms the fundamental, incarnational truth that pleasure, even bodily pleasure, is good. Second, he teaches us that both pleasure and the ascetic renunciation of pleasure need to be *reasonably ordered* lest we suffer a "dullness of wit," "derangement of appetite," or diminution of our strength for service—any of which can interfere with the harmoniousness and happiness of our living (IIaIIae, 148, 6). Third, he urges us to exercise a holistic care for our bodily health as integrally related to our spiritual well-being. Fourth, he reminds us that attention to the needs of our neighbors should duly moderate attention to our own indulgences and austerities. And finally, he insists that proper orientation of our priorities should always be our most serious theological concern, such that preoccupation with what we do or do not eat never be allowed to override the central purpose of our lives: to rejoice in the abundant gifts of God, and to love the Giver with all our heart, soul, mind, and strength.

HOLY ANOREXICS

When I read Gregory the Great, I feel gently and pastorally admonished, drawn into reflection about the unseemly excesses of my own life. When I read the penitential handbooks, I feel intrigued, admitted into the private concerns and practices of an era so unlike, yet so like, my own. When I read Thomas Aquinas, I feel soothed—as if someone has taken all the clutter and jumble of note cards and random ideas strewn across my desk, and sorted them into tidy piles for me, showing me clarity and pattern where before there had been only cobwebs and confusion. In a word, when I read the *Summa*, I feel *taught*—patiently, meticulously, and lucidly instructed by a master teacher, a *doctor angelicus*, as Thomas has aptly been named by generations of grateful students.

When I turn to the next and last body of literature which we shall sample in our historical digest of foundational Christian attitudes toward eating, I find myself fascinated—both attracted and repelled by attitudes which sound simultaneously resonant and sharply dissonant with my own experiences. I refer to the writings of those medieval women who approach sanctity through feats of extraordinary food asceticism: the "holy anorexics," as they have been labeled.[36] I feel a kinship with these women, in part simply because they *are* women, whereas the vast majority of texts we have investigated thus far have been written primarily by and for men. I feel a kinship with these women because struggles with food form a central motif in their, as in my own, living. Food *means* something to these women; it is anything but a trivial issue for them (and even they must put up with an occasionally curling lip from their confessors). Yet, *what* food means to them stands in striking contrast to the meanings food acquires in the struggles of anorexics and bulimics, compulsive eaters and compulsive dieters in the modern world. The contrasts are telling on both sides of the divide—telling in terms of what we and they actually do value, and in terms of what might be of healthier, holier value in our living. Medievals and moderns, sisters and strangers, we have much to learn from each other.

One of the medieval women recently labeled a "holy anorexic" by historical scholars bears another more traditional and official title: the Dominican tertiary Catherine of Siena, like the Dominican friar Thomas Aquinas before her, is known as a *doctor* or teacher of the Church. Large and lumbering, Thomas is legendary for his girth. Small and spirited, Catherine is legendary in her own day (if virtually unknown in ours) for her emaciation.

At the age of fifteen, shortly after the death of an older sister, Catherine undertakes a rigorous program of self-denial, restricting her diet to raw vegetables, bread, and water—and in a short period of time, losing half her body weight. After joining the Sisters of Penance, a group of lay women affiliated with the Dominican Order but living in the world rather than in cloistered retreat, she increases her food austerities. She stops eating bread, and lives on water and bitter herbs which she chews and then spits out before swallowing. As Raymond of Capua, her confessor and biographer describes her practices:

> Her stomach could digest nothing . . . therefore anything she in-gested needed to exit by the same way it entered, otherwise it caused her acute pain and swelling of her entire body. The holy virgin swallowed nothing of the herbs and things she chewed; nevertheless, because it was impossible to avoid some crumb of food or juice descending into her stomach . . . she was constrained every day to vomit what she had eaten. To do this she regularly and with great pain inserted stalks of fennel . . . into her stomach.[37]

Catherine lives this way from her mid-twenties until her early thirties, at which time she also renounces drinking water. Her desire is to subsist on the nourishment of the eucharist alone, and to do the most severe penance she can for the ills of a seriously troubled Church. Her austerities lead to a total physical collapse, convulsions, perhaps even a coma. Although she ends her complete hunger strike in February of 1380, her body has suffered irrecoverably. She dies three months later from the effects of her self-starvation, wracked with excruciating stomach pains but blessed with spiritual serenity.

Food clearly *means* something in the life of this fourteenth-century theologian, spiritual adviser, mystic, and highly venerated miracle-worker; it means enough to Catherine that she insists on depriving herself of it, even unto death. The question is, *what* exactly do food and food deprivation mean to this medieval "anorexic" and the many others like her in the twelfth through the seventeenth centuries? And further, what can we in the late twentieth century learn from these women about appropriate and inappropriate ways to order our food lives in an increasingly eating-disordered society?

Like any fundamental and powerful symbol, that of food is multiply-determined, overdetermined. At one level, food means "forbidden fruit," it means sinful desiring, it means a dangerous incitement to other lusts of the flesh. Many of the patristic traditions, still alive in the Middle Ages, teach—as we have seen—that Adam's first sin is gluttony, and that his provocation to this sin comes from the woman. Such a significant linkage of images is not lost on the "holy anorexics." When Catherine of Siena is chastised by an adviser for her extraordinary abstinence, she responds to him by letter, saying that her inability to eat is not the result of "a demonic siege and self-deception," but rather a gift from "God who by a most singular mercy allowed me to correct the vice of gluttony."[38] In her *Dialogue*, she describes the eucharist as a divine gift to replace "heavy physical bread," the eating of which can arouse gluttony and lust.[39]

Still, Carolyn Bynum concludes from her extensive research that gluttony is more a theme in the writings of medieval men than in those of women. In general, she notes, "male [monastic] houses were both wealthier and larger than female houses, and gluttony was, in fact, a greater possibility and, therefore, temptation."[40] For women, food-related practices do not revolve so much around mastery of the temptation to excess, but rather around a whole matrix of further meanings: charity, nurture, control, eucharistic fervor, identification with the sufferings of Christ. These meanings shock and surprise and speak to us as modern readers in telling fashion.

Food means charity, nurture, and control. Medieval religious women live out the insight, central to Gregory the Great's pastoral theology, that fasting avails little as an expression of piety unless it is coupled with feeding the poor. They enact this ideal, however, in surprising ways. Not only do they feed others by givings alms or by working wonders of food multiplication; as women, they also feed others with their own bodies which (in life or in death) miraculously exude milk, oil, honey, healing liquids. Such acts of prototypically feminine maternal nurturing work in paradoxical ways to undermine patriarchal notions of femininity. The priestly role which is denied women in life accrues to them in death when they reappear in visions, offering the chalice of communion to nourish their followers.

The economic role which is denied women by society, they arrogate to themselves, liberally and deliberately dispensing the one resource over which they have some control: food. Stories abound of women who deplete their families' larders in giving to the poor, as a gesture of charity and a gesture of revolt against familial materialism (and even an attempt to appear undesirable to would-be suitors!). Deprived of property and of legal rights, women have very little which is theirs to give up in ascetic denial, other than food. Refusal to eat thus becomes a key ingredient in female efforts to forge a religious identity. Fasting serves paradoxically as a renunciation of control, leaving the responsibility for sustenance to God, and an exercise of control, assuming roles of charity, self-sacrifice, and self-assertion which are otherwise withheld from women in the medieval world.

In addition to charity, nurture, and control, food also means eucharistic fervor for the holy anorexics. Like Catherine of Siena, many of them desire to eat nothing but the host, the communion wafer. When for various reasons the eucharist is unavailable to them, they have visions in which they are fed by Christ himself: from an outstretched chalice, from his blood, even from his breast. Margaret Miles insists that we should not overlook the manner in which fasting actually serves to create the intense affective and physiological state through which such visions become possible.[41] Carolyn Bynum reminds us (as Roy Porter and Piero Camporesi have already done) that food assumes an immense importance in the uncertain economy of the Middle Ages, so much so that eating makes sense as "the most basic and literal way of encountering God."[42] The eucharist provides a rich occasion for "eating God": for touching, tasting, communing with, and literally incorporating the divine Beloved. When Catherine of Siena partakes of the communion for which she hungers, "a very torrent of heavenly graces" so floods her soul that they "[brim] over upon her body also, checking the flow of its vital juices, and so altering the action of her stomach that it [can] no longer assimilate [other] food."[43] Eucharistic fervor clearly runs as a highly charged current through the eating practices, the piety, and the passion of "holy anorexics."

A final complex of meanings attaching to food-related practices in holy anorexia involves the theme of identification with the sufferings of Christ: *imitatio Christi*. This is the theme whose enactment becomes most shocking to modern perceptions. Catherine of Siena so wants to mortify her own flesh in sympathy with the suffering of her savior that she not only carries the penance of fasting to life-threatening extremes; she further forces herself to drink a ladel full of pus from the suppurating breast sores of a woman she is tending. Other "holy anorexics" perform similar acts, trying to crucify their bodily sensations of pleasure or revulsion by eating lice, maggots, and scabs or drinking water in which they have bathed the wounds of lepers. If there is much that is admirable in the fervid devotion of these women, there is also much that is, at least to modern readers, appalling.

Some of the appalling mortifications of the flesh practiced by these medieval women can be explained as a counter-cultural reaction: just as the desert fathers of the fourth century sought an "other-worldly" asceticism in self-martyring response to the decadence of the Greco-Roman world, so the holy anorexics of the fourteenth century seek a staunch discipline in response to growing laxity within the medieval Church. Some of these mortifications can be traced to internalized misogyny: to an incorporation of the widely taught image of woman as temptress and femaleness as fleshly weakness in need of rigorous mastery. Many of these self-mortifying behaviors can be understood as pious and positive efforts (however strange or even repugnant to us) at paradoxically gaining a measure of self-control and self-definition in an over-whelmingly patriarchal society. But these efforts at interpretation still do not completely bridge the chasm between medieval and modern expressions of selfhood or of sanctity. Fascinating though they be, the "holy anorexics" remain resolutely strangers to us.

Yet, these medieval holy women are also our sisters. Even as they show us the literally morbid extremes to which an *imitatio* of suffering can be taken, they also show us the vibrant possibilities of a life in which the smallest daily acts contribute to an overall orientation of service and devotion to the divine Beloved, a life in which food as an essential ingredient of dailiness is anything but a trivial issue. In their struggles with food, these women remind us, at least at some levels, of ourselves. Catherine of Siena and Ellen West, different though they be, both find powerful meaning for their lives in self-imposed dietary regimens. Not content with mediocrity, they both seek to become exceptional. Medieval and modern, the patterns of their eating bear striking similarities to one another, even as the purposes animating their unusual practices reveal both convergent and divergent features.

The pattern of "holy anorexia" reveals noteworthy parallels with modern-day eating disorders. Both phenomena are charac-terized by symptoms which begin or escalate in early adolescence. Despite a depletion of bodily resources through frequent fasting or purging, both holy anorexia and anorexia nervosa call forth sleepless nights, perfectionism, and frenetic activity, often involv-ing the insistent preparation of food for others. Medievals and moderns both seem to lose the ability to read and interpret normal bodily sensations of hunger or satiation. Body concepts become distorted: consuming the slightest amount of food pro-motes horrible sensations of swelling; intense feelings of guilt, nausea, and self-loathing follow. While claiming an extraordinar-ily sparse regimen and an inability to keep down any but the most minimal quantities of food, both medieval fasters and modern dieters get caught up in patterns of secretive, compensatory gorging. Attempts at rigorous deprivation provoke obsessive pre-occupation with thoughts of food. A preemptive focus on eating or not eating diffuses other potentially threatening issues—issues of sexuality and of relationships, in particular. Both medievals and moderns find that their peculiar dietary practices put them into conflict with their families or communities. Either wittingly or unwittingly, the "sufferers" of both eras manipulate this conflict to achieve a sense of personal strength, selfhood, and control.

In a patriarchal society—like that of the fourteenth, or of the twentieth century, for that matter—such an achievement stands as no mean feat. It discloses both convergent and divergent features in the purposes animating the holy anorexic and the secular dieter. Each uses her food life in search of approbation and power in the coinage of the realm she inhabits. Pursuing the coin of spiritual status, the medieval woman engages in rigorously correlated practices of austerity and almsgiving. Her modern counterpart counts calories, exercises obsessively, or engages in compensatory rituals of secret gorging and painful purging in pursuit of the coin of physical attractiveness and social acceptability. Both sets of efforts demand considerable self-denial; neither set expresses an ability to appreciate or savor incarnational pleasure.

Nevertheless, in spite of all its limitations and all its potential morbidity, the medieval goal still seems more richly nuanced than our own. For Catherine of Siena and her contemporaries, food consists of far more than calories. Indeed, it participates in a whole matrix of meanings relating to nurture, charity, eucharistic piety, and redemptive suffering. For Catherine and her kindred, the body which feeds and fasts does not stand as an individual commodity in a marketplace where personal appearance measures ultimate worth. Rather, the body figures as part of a corporate reality, a *corpus Christi*, which cries out for communal care and responsibility. For both medieval and modern women—more so than for men of either era—food bears the highly charged image of the fruit which is forbidden, and fleshliness carries the particular weight of a wickedness which must be subdued. Yet, for the holy anorexic, the renunciation of food and fleshliness occurs for the sake of an ulterior godliness. For the modern woman, sadly, thinness becomes a god unto itself.

AFTER TASTE

In the next course of our movable feast, we will look further at the processes through which thinness comes to be placed so close to godliness in the modern system of values. For now, however, we would do well to pause a moment to assimilate the smorgasbord of traditional sources which we have just been sampling.

We began this "historical digest" with a series of guiding questions related to foundational Christian teachings about problematic eating, which are generally contained under the rubric of gluttony within listings of the "seven deadly sins." Our questions can be re-framed under three headings. First, what exactly is gluttony, as traditionally understood, and why has it been labeled "sinful"? Second, is this label exclusively pertinent to monastic, "other-worldly" ascetic attitudes, or does it convey some wisdom about the appropriate ordering of our "this-worldly" bodily living? Third, what relationship links traditional conceptions of gluttony to the modern phenomena of eating disorders?

We have seen that gluttony, within the Christian tradition, has nothing to do with girth, with matters of body shape or size. Rather, it concerns patterns of consumption—particularly, patterns of eating and drinking which put acquisitiveness and ingestion above all other values. For the glutton, whether he or she be fat or thin, food becomes more important than community, than charity, than health, than gratitude for the savory gifts of God's creation. Like its correlated sin of excessive abstemiousness, gluttony is sinful insofar as it marks a mis-orientation of priorities—one which turns exclusively inward to the self and fails to attend appreciatively to any transcendent value.

Although the predominant condemnations of gluttony as a "deadly sin" arise in monastic literature of the fourth Christian century, the prohibition of immoderate consumption is also appropriate to life outside the monastery and within the world. Biblical texts decry any idolatry of food (making a god of the belly) or of dietary practice (making a god of any self-righteous regimen). Pastoral, penitential, and scholastic texts repeat the biblical teachings of balance, arguing that the celebration of feasts is as important as the discipline of fasting, and insisting that the dullness of "insensibility" is as much to be shunned as the dangers of immoderation.

When we move from the context of male theological writings about gluttony from the fourth through thirteenth centuries to that of female attempts to live out patterns of personal holiness in the medieval period, we move to a setting that more and more closely approximates the modern context of eating disorders. Holy anorexia bears remarkable phenomenological parallels to twentieth-century anorexia and bulimia. Both sets of behaviors fear food and fleshliness as embodiments of ensnaring temptation. Both seek personal power and control, at the price of rigid self-denial. The medieval woman struggles with food because she would be holy; the modern woman, because she would be beautiful. In either case, eating serves as the emblem of the primordial sin: the sin of taking too much for oneself, taking too much into oneself. Catherine of Siena and Ellen West bear this in common with Eve, the mother of all living. For women particularly, to take, and touch, and taste (*sapere*) is to seek a fearsome, forbidden wisdom (*sapientia*). Better that we waste our bodies and our energies in starving and purging ourselves. Better that we seek holiness through emaciation, or even that we prostrate ourselves before a pseudo-god of thinness.

Or is it? To such critical ruminations, we now turn.

The God of Thinness

THE AMBIVALENCE OF EVE

To taste (*sapere*) is to risk gaining wisdom (*sapientia*). Some tasting—like some wisdom—is dangerous. This is the lesson of Eve, the lesson of the forbidden fruit. I am a daughter of Eve.

A daughter of Eve, I am also a sister of Catherine of Siena and Ellen West. The cries of these women, and so many like them (like *us*), compel me to qualify my second sentence above: some, *but not all*, tasting is dangerous. A deep ambivalence haunts the story of Eve, of woman, of humans confronting the pleasures and dangers of appetite. It is an ambivalence which I as a feminist theologian discern in theory, and which I as a woman in recovery from an eating disorder duplicate daily in practice. As a feminist, some days I read the Eden story as a patriarchal ploy intended (consciously or otherwise) to alienate human beings from the forbidding fruits of femaleness and the flesh, from a full-bodied tasting that might serve to make us wise. Other days, I read the Eden story as an insightful diagnosis: there *are* perils to taking into ourselves that which we are not prepared to handle; some tasting *is* hazardous to our spiritual and physical health. As a recovering bulimic, some days I think I should simply relax, take pleasure in food, and let my body assume the contours that it will. Other days, I think if I dared to relax, my voraciousness would overwhelm me. On such days, I sob to myself (uncomfortable as it is to confess it): "I would rather be dead than out of control. I would rather be dead than fat."

At one level, the Eve story—at least as traditionally interpreted—does work toward the joint repression of woman (the "temptress") and of appetite (the temptation). A feminist reading of this story (such as that done by Kim Chernin in her richly evocative book *Reinventing Eve*) focuses on the patriarchal ploys at work in such repression.[1] Chernin observes that in many pre-biblical cultures (indeed, in Canaanite cultures contemporaneous with the development of the Hebrew scriptures and in gnostic sects contemporaneous with the recording of the Christian canon), a powerful Mother Goddess reigns in place of or in consort with a Father God. This life-and-food-giving Mother is often associated with a fruit tree: magic peach trees for the Great Mother Hsi Wang Mu in China, a golden apple tree for the Goddess Hera in Greece, a fig tree for the Babylonian Ishtar (156). Even as the emblem of the Goddess is often a fruit tree, so Her emissary is often a serpent. In ancient Sumaria, the scribe of heaven takes the form of a snake; in Greek mythology, the World Egg is formed when Eurynome is impregnated by the serpent Ophion. Chernin concludes: "The serpent in these old tales is the Goddess Herself . . . and sometimes, in later stories, the snake [is] regarded as . . . an Instructor, who comes to teach and inform (155)."

If the fruit tree stands mythically for the pre-patriarchal Mother, and the snake for Her primordial wisdom, then the Hebraic taboo on the fruit of the tree at the center of Eden takes on a new symbolic resonance. For a feminist reading of the Genesis narrative, the prohibition against this fruit conceals a fear that eating of it might reunite us with the nurturing Mother, thereby teaching us that the masculine Yahweh does not reign aloof and supreme. For a feminist reading, the serpent of the Hebraic tale is depicted as demonic because it attempts to lead humans back to the Goddess. For a feminist reading, when Eve listens to the serpent, she hears beneath its words the whisper of a primal and visceral knowledge: to be female is not to be weak, but rather to be strong; not to be seductive, but rather to be re-source-full (filled as the Source of birth and of being). In the utterance of the serpent and the taste of the fruit, Eve approaches a revolutionary recognition: that she as a woman can be called a "mother of all living" precisely because she is a daughter of the Great Mother Herself.

I confess that there are times when this feminist reading speaks powerfully to me. In its affirmation of food and fecundity and femaleness and the flesh, it *gives me back my appetite*. It affirms a world in which touching and tasting are *good*, and all eating is feasting at the breast of the Mother. As a feminist theologian who has seen the fierce misogyny produced by traditional interpretations of Eve as "temptress," I am heartened by an intepretation which views her as a seeker of "Mother wit." As a compulsive dieter who has internalized the misogyny of my religious tradition in the form of disgust at my own hungering female body, I find comfort in the wise whispers of the serpent who tells me it is permitted to take, eat, and enjoy.

But the human story, the Adam and Eve story, is an ambivalent one, and this feminist reading seems to me to omit one side of the ambivalence. While empowering in its conjoined celebrations of fruit, flesh, and femaleness, an interpretation such as Chernin's overlooks the sobering point which is crucial to the biblical narrative: some tasting *is* dangerous. *Not all* tasting is dangerous, and on this score the feminist reading yields a helpful corrective to generations of anti-pleasure bias in appropriations of the Eden narrative. But such a bias, at its root, is also anti-biblical: all *but one* of the fruit trees of Eden are delightful to the eye and pleasing to the taste and perfectly legitimate to enjoy. Applauding enjoyment, the myth-makers of Genesis also raise an important caution: there *is* that which we consume to our peril.

I know the truth of this caution both theoretically and practically—as a theological proponent of the tragic reality of *sin* and as a personal sufferer of the sin-filled experience of voracious appetite. I know that I do reach beyond myself for privileges, powers, and pleasures—"forbidden fruits"—which I am not wise enough to handle. I know that the primal act of eating provides a palpable prototype for any act in which I take eagerly from another with thought only for myself. I know that my appetites can run riot, numbing me to consequences beyond the present moment of frantic consumption. I know, in short, that I am a sinner: an outcast from the garden of harmonious happiness, a daughter of my human and fallen foremother Eve.

And I am a sister of Catherine of Siena and of Ellen West—but in significantly different ways. Both Catherine and Ellen bear the legacy of Eve: both fear food as ensnaring and seek release from temptation through rigorous appetite control. Catherine desires to be thin as a symbol of holiness, as an imitation of the hungering and suffering of Christ. Ellen desires slenderness for more secular reasons. When Catherine stops eating and drinking altogether in her early thirties, it becomes clear that she is seeking not only identification but *reunion* with her crucified Lord—that she would rather be dead than living. While there may be some pathological resonance to her intense self-mortification, there is undeniable piety to it as well. When Ellen West dreads eating and not eating, and obsesses over gaining and losing weight, the system of values which shapes her struggle is different from Catherine's and much closer to my own. Ellen West would rather be dead than fat.

I know that feeling. So, alas, do many other women and men in contemporary American society. Painful as it is, embarrassing as it is, such a feeling attests to a dramatic shift in societal values. From the story of Eve to the *legenda* of Catherine of Siena to the case study of Ellen West, we have moved in western culture from a prohibition against tasting a single forbidden fruit to a squeamishness about tasting in general. We have moved from a set of admonitions against gluttony to a set of prejudices against fatness. We have moved from profound issues of appropriation of the goods of the earth to superficial issues of personal appearance. Such moves are costly.

This chapter explores the origins and nature of the costs entailed in our shift in focus from gluttony to girth and from consumption to cosmetics. It does so by investigating two interdependent phenomena: the emergence of "thinness" as a contemporary cultural idol, and the development of "weightism" as a set of discriminatory attitudes and practices aimed against those who do not conform to the thinness norm. A third and related phenomenon, which will carry us into the next chapter, is the tension between explanatory frameworks which account for fatness as given or as chosen, as a matter of medical or of moral import. To explore these phenomena is not only to assess critically the values of contemporary culture; it is also to seek a theoretical and practical basis for assuaging the pains of compulsive eating, compulsive dieting, and fat-phobic self-disgust.

THE GOD OF THINNESS

Pleasingly Plump and Suspiciously Slim

Statues of the Goddess from ancient Malta depict her as *huge*. She is as wide as she is high. Rolls upon rolls of flesh billow down her abdomen. Her thighs and upper arms are like tree trunks, sturdy and solid. She conveys a combined image of nurturing comfort and no-nonsense power. The contemporary feminist artist Maud Morgan has done a painting of the impressive form of this goddess. She titles her painting "I'd Like to Go to Malta."[2] Yes. I understand.

In 1825, Jean Anthelme Brillat-Savarin published a comprehensive analysis of appetite in his (literal) magnum opus, *The Physiology of Taste*. In it, he opines, "classical plumpness . . . has always charmed man's eyes" and "every thin woman wants to grow plump." Indeed, he continues:

> Thinness is a horrible calamity for women: beauty to them is more than life itself, and it consists above all of the roundness of their forms. . . . A scrawny woman, no matter how pretty she may look, loses something of her charm with every fastening she undoes.[3]

Sometimes I'd like to go to early nineteenth-century France!

Countless further examples could be adduced to illustrate the point that a certain amplitude, especially in women, has not always been disparaged. The Flemish Renaissance painter Rubens is celebrated for creating female figures which overflow with the lushness of softly abundant flesh. The seventeenth-century English poet John Dryden has his Maiden Queen proudly announce: "I am resolved to grow fat, and look young till forty."[4] There are tribes in Eastern Nigeria even today which seclude young women in huts, feeding them lavishly and forbidding them exercise so that they may be appropriately fattened for marriage. There are

Polynesian cultures which revere women whose regal proportions swell to 300 or more pounds.[5] Modern American fat-phobia is clearly a historically and culturally conditioned phenomenon.

Just as fatness has not always been scorned, so slenderness has not always been idealized (as Brillat-Savarin's provocative depiction of the "scrawny woman" implies). Indeed, for many centuries prior to our own—and for cultures marked by economic scarcity rather than abundance—thinness betrays poverty and ill health while stoutness boasts prosperity and vigor. Indeed, it is startling (if just a bit gratifying) to discover that for generations whose assumptions differ from our own, *gluttony* is as readily identified with thinness as with corpulence! An illuminated fourteenth-century manuscript of the "Pilgrimage of Human Life" portrays Gluttony as a stick-straight figure with a feed bag strapped around his neck.[6] In a medieval sermon, Rypon denounces gluttony as a particularly "perilous" sin, in part because "excess of mete and of drynke wastyth a mannys body . . . and megryth [emaciates] him with longe sykness."[7]

The notion seems bizarre: eating to excess "wastes" and emaciates our bodies; gluttony makes us too thin! Yet, there is perhaps no better way of flushing out the peculiar prejudices of our own worldview than that of attending to those features of earlier perspectives which sound the strangest to our hearing. Why do we so unquestioningly assume that gluttony makes us fat (or that fatness means we are gluttonous), except for the fact that our culture takes it as a given that fat is bad and thin is good, even virtuous?

In fact, the ear-opening notion that gluttony emaciates rather than engorges the body has a persistent history. In the early 1800s in the United States, dietary reformers like Sylvester Graham—inventer of the highly nutritious Graham cracker (really!)—argue that gluttonous consumption leads to "dyspepsia"—a general rubric for gastrointestinal disturbance—which in turn leads to excessive thinness.[8] The American diet of the nineteenth century astounds European visitors by its abundance of meat and fat; the speed with which Americans eat is equally appalling to foreign observers. But the result of such seeming indiscretions is not girth; it is indigestion. According to the popular wisdom of the era, food which has been minimally chewed or savored can be only minimally assimilated. Thus, eating overly eagerly (the form of gluttony which Gregory and Thomas would have labeled as eating *ardenter*) supposedly prevents the distribution of flesh and nutrients to bodily tissues.

And dangerously so. Even through the early years of the twentieth century in the United States, a thin body equates to an undernourished and an unhealthy one. Dreaded afflictions like pneumonia and tuberculosis are associated with emaciation; children who have "a good reservoir of fat" seem better able to withstand infectious diseases. "Neurasthenia," a purported disease of nervous exhaustion brought on by the "frantic pace" of late nineteenth-century civilization, results from excessive worry and inadequate digestion. The recommended antidote (how strange this sounds to us): a sufficiency of fat in the bloodstream! Indeed, the ills of insufficient fat are so widely assumed that insurance companies up into the early 1900s screen underweight applicants more stringently than they do those who are healthily stout. As late as 1926, a former president of the American Medical Association, Dr. Woods Hutchinson, charitably refers to fat as "one of the most peaceable, useful, and law-abiding of our tissues"![9]

Technology and a "Streamlined" Ideal

How times change! Two recent books meticulously chronicle those changes over the past two centuries which have moved American society from a suspicion of thinness to a loathing of fat. In *Never Satisfied*, Hillel Schwartz serves up a rich and entertaining history of diets, with all their accompanying fantasies, fetishes, and paraphernalia. In *Never Too Thin*, Roberta Pollack Seid analyzes in intriguing detail such intertwined phenomena as advertising, fashion, and physical fitness programs in order to uncover the roots of our current thinness obsession. Together, Schwartz and Seid provide a smorgasbord of source materials for coming to appreciate the historic shift in attitudes from fat-approbation to fat-phobia.

This attitudinal shift reveals an interesting interplay between the ideology and the artifacts of the technological revolution sweeping through American society since the early 1800s. The growth of industry, abetted by technology, puts a premium on *streamlining* and efficiency. At the turn of the twentieth century, automobiles and airplanes, modern dance and motion pictures, mechanization and mass production, all join forces in shaping a new "kinaesthetic ideal"—one that celebrates speed, energy, and mastery of nature, including mastery of the human body. Home economics, with a freshly expert focus on nutrition, is emerging as a science. National economics is wrestling for the first time with problems caused by overabundance—*glut*—and a need for regulation. By the 1920s, fashion has moved away from voluminous skirts to more severe tailoring, promoting a chic "kinetic silhouette" which accentuates spare and slender lines. In factory, home, and marketplace—as well as in body shape and clothing style—*excess* comes increasingly to appear as irresponsible waste. Schwartz summarizes this emergent ideology: "Between 1880 and 1920," he writes, "gluttony (freed from its association with thinness) would be bound to fatness, [and] fatness to inefficiency."[10] Economy of form and economy of movement are becoming cultural ideals. Thinness is on its way to becoming a cultural idol.

In tandem with the ideology of the technological revolution, assorted artifacts of that revolution promote a new preoccupation with body shape and size. Items that we take for granted in the dailiness of our living are just becoming current in the early decades of this century. Take ready-to-wear clothing, for example. Idiosyncratic body measurements are less apparent when clothing is made to specification at home (for the poor) or by personal tailors (for the wealthy). By way of unfortunate contrast, the availability of ready-made garments reinforces a notion that there are "standard" and "correct" body sizes. And even these sizes are subject to vary with the ever-slimmer dictates of the ever-expanding fashion and beauty industries. In the 1930s, the smallest size regularly stocked in women's dress shops is a 12 or 14; by the mid-1950s, a 14 or 16 is the *largest* size readily available![11]

Or for another example, take bathroom scales (take mine: please!). Such instruments of self-scrutiny are commonplace in American homes today; some of us even own several different models, because one of them can usually be counted on to weigh us "lower" than the others do. In the 1990s, rituals of self-weighing vary from once a month or so for the relatively blasé to once every hour or after every meal for the seriously size-obsessed. Yet, standardized scales for use in annual medical examinations are only introduced in the 1890s; penny scales for public weighing become popular in the 1920s and 1930s; and sales of home scales do not really take off (so to speak) until the 1950s. As the ideal of beauty becomes progressively streamlined, the mechanism for measuring "beauty" becomes increasingly abstract. Science and technology create in the scale a device which, with one simple number, can be used to determine a person's presumed levels of health, fitness, attractiveness, social acceptability, and self-satisfaction.[12]

Yet another abstraction emergent from turn-of-the-century developments in science has a profound impact on the emergent cult of slenderness: the calorie. As home economics and nutrition take on scientific status, food comes to be measured in terms of its productivity as fuel for the body-machine. From computing in the 1880s the numbers of calories expended in various activities, researchers move in the early 1900s to recommending dietary standards for the nation through the U.S. Department of Agriculture. When the concept of the calorie is introduced to the general public, it initially has positive connotations: advertisers tout their products as "rich in energizing calories." Even into the 1940s, 80% of housewives responding to a Gallup poll cannot distinguish between a vitamin and a calorie: both, after all, are scientific units measuring the efficacy of food-as-fuel. But by the early 1950s, what Roberta Pollack Seid labels as "the war on fat" begins in earnest, and calories acquire both fame and infamy as public enemies in the burgeoning battle.[13]

Fashion and Fitness

Clothing sizes, bathroom scales, and calories—the three most common opponents in the weight-and-diet obsessiveness of the late 1900s—all début in the earlier decades of this very century as the result of applied advances in science and technology. Fashion advertising and the promotion of physical fitness further shape the skeleton of factors serving to buttress the thinness ideal.

THE GOD OF THINNESS

It would be hard to overestimate the impact of the fashion industry on the body-size obsessions of contemporary society. The exaltation of slenderness seems to arrive in the United States in three ever-widening waves. The first wave ripples onto our shores in the 1820s. The "Steel Engraving Lady" of fashion magazine illustrations is delicate and willowy; she depicts the kind of ethereality celebrated in the first flush of imported European Romanticism. In dance, women first go on point around the 1830s, giving artistic expression to ideals of otherworldly lightness and refinement. But not all American women can be ballerinas, or even attend the ballet. And even the circulation of *Godey's Lady Book* is limited to a relatively elite few. The dainty ideal of femininity thus gives way by the 1850s to a more mature and substantial image of womanhood.[14]

The second wave of fashionable slenderness crests in the 1930s, again imported from Europe—this time, from the work of Paris designer Paul Poiret and his celebration of the sleek silhouette. Newspapers and the newly developing film industry carry such dictates of style to an ever more populous audience. Technology now makes it possible for photographs of actual models (who could ostensibly be imitated by other "real women") to take the place of steel engravings in women's magazines. Writers for *Vogue* and *Ladies' Home Journal* applaud slim lines and deride excessive flesh as "awkward" and "untidy." An article in *Fortune* in 1936 refers, with no particular dismay, to the use of laxatives and emetics as a dieting technique which has "captured the American mind." The body-shaping which was once performed by skillful tailoring and strategic undergarments must now be provided by the body itself. Under the flapper's skimpy and skimming sheath, there is little place for inadequacies or over-adequacies to hide.[15]

As the flapper cedes her place to Rosie the Riveter, however, images of women—and tastes in fashion—change once again. Food shortages brought on by the Great Depression and World War II make dieting and purging seem irrelevant if not ridiculous. There are more important things to worry about. Such a statement is not to trivialize weight-related concerns (I watch carefully to keep my own lip from curling). It is, however, to emphasize that such concerns are culture-bound: bound to an economic context of relative plenty; bound to an ideological context in which clear adversaries have been supplanted by a vague, internalized discontent, and clear sources of meaning have vanished, leaving little in their wake but the small compensations of a search for self-esteem.

Into such a context in post-World War II America surges the third wave of fashionable thinness, indisputably the most widespread, long-lasting, and ultimately devastating of them all. *Fortune* magazine may comment on dieting and purging in the 1930s, but it is in the 1980s and 1990s that eating aberrations reach epidemic proportions. Multiple factors figure in this third wave, but it has one outstanding, if diminutive, figurehead—again an import. Her name is Twiggy.

Aged seventeen, standing 5′7½″ and weighing only 91 pounds, the British model Twiggy becomes not just the the aesthetic ideal for other teen-aged girls in the 1960s (which would be sad enough), but that for women of all ages. In a combined abhorrence of fat and of aging, American women enter into the feverish pursuit of weight loss as a means of insuring perpetual youth (or at least a youthful appearance). Feminist analysts have gone so far as to suggest a patriarchal conspiracy behind this fashion trend which diverts women's energies into seeking a childish, even waif-like appearance at a point in history when they are finally threatening to storm the bastions of traditional male power.[16] Whether witting or not, the diversion works. In the presence of a mass media blitz of girl-woman images, with fashion models and Miss America contestants growing thinner year after year; in the absence of any strongly countervailing images of what confers personal attractiveness or meaning or worth, more and more women get sucked into arduous and utimately self-defeating battles with their own (our own) bodies. We deflect our attention into obsessive self-scrutiny: weighing and measuring our food, weighing and measuring ourselves, hating our appearance, hating our need for and resistance to discipline, hating our self-hatred. Some days, it seems, we have little strength left for anything else. As Naomi Wolf has aptly concluded, "Dieting is the most potent political sedative in women's history."[17] Amen. The "god of thinness" demands a deadening tribute which we would be loath to lay before any other altar.

Of course, the fashion industry alone cannot be blamed for the construction of this seductive altar, and the burden of responsibility for our current diet and weight obsessions cannot be laid solely on the skinny shoulders of one seventeen-year-old fashion model. From the 1950s forward, the new industry of fitness joins forces with that of fashion in promoting a slender ideal. As a result, popular thinking in the U.S. increasingly links thinness not simply to beauty, but also to health—and thereby, momentously, to virtue.

If Twiggy stands as the icon for the fashionable thinness movement, the Metropolitan Life Insurance Company [MLIC] aptly symbolizes the movement which moralizes the image of thin-as-fit (and in so doing, demoralizes "overweight" people across the land). In fact, the very category of "*over*weight" demands a concept of normal or appropriate or "ideal" weight that one can be "over"—a concept developed by insurance companies on the assumption that certain weights correlate with better health (and a better insurance risk!). The concept itself has at least a century-old history, but its powerful popularization dates to a 1951 report by Louis I. Dublin of the MLIC to the American Medical Association, claiming succinctly that "Overweight Shortens Life" and defining overweight as a mere 10% above the charted "ideal."[18]

With health and longevity (as well as fashionable clothing and low insurance premiums) at stake, Americans begin using our new knowledge of calories to diet in earnest. The ideology of the body-as-machine spawns a mentality of mathematical control: to store less fat, we are instructed to consume less fuel, in a simple 3500-to-one calorie-to-pound ratio. In the 1950s, the "low-cal" industry takes off (again, so to speak), with Metrecal (remember?) and Tillie Lewis products (yes, Virginia, there really is a Tillie Lewis, voted Business Woman of the Year in 1952).[19] Nor is cutting down on the number of calories we eat sufficient in the fight for life, loveliness, and a lissome figure. Medical experts further decry modern, sedentary lifestyles as contributing to the "overweight" and ill health of American society. Exercising becomes *de rigueur*. In 1965, the first chart depicting the numbers of calories burned up in various forms of physical activity appears. Jogging catches on. "Aerobics" becomes a household word.[20]

And beneath it all runs a swift current of evangelical fervor. If the the body is a machine which can be streamlined by a mathematical process of consuming less and expending more, then weight loss should be a simple matter of control and weight gain must betray a lack of discipline—whether the outgrowth of obstinacy, laziness, blatant self-indulgence, or blind ignorance of the perils of fat. In a country bred on Puritan ideals, none of these attributes can be tolerated. The prescribed antidote (where but in America?): the power of positive thinking. Jack LaLanne, calisthenics coach and aerobics apostle, takes television audiences by storm in the 1950s and 1960s as a kind of "Norman Vincent Peale with muscles." He even compares himself to evangelist Billy Graham ("He puts people in shape for the hereafter, and I get them fit for the here and now").[21] LaLanne follows a significant legacy: Sylvester Graham (Presbyterian minister of the mid-1800s, itinerant preacher, promoter of dietary righteousness in the form of pure fruits and vegetables and "unbolted wheat bread" or Graham crackers); John Harvey Kellogg (Seventh Day Adventist of the late 1800s to early 1900s and director of the Adventist sanitarium in Battle Creek, Michigan; elder brother to the inventer of corn flakes and All-Bran; promoter of "sensitive colon conscience" and excoriator of sluggish bowels).[22] For generations, Americans have found ourselves swept up by the exhortations of health and fitness evangelists.

What is new in the past three decades of the twentieth century is the single-minded focus on *fat* in these exhortations. If once upon a time, temperance (marked by hygienic eating and efficient digesting) appeared close to godliness, now a trim waistline assumes that place of honor. Sylvester Graham, John Harvey Kellogg, and even Jack LaLanne are all preeminently concerned with the *processes* by which we might move from dyspepsia, neurasthenia, and general puniness to robust health; in more recent decades, we are more narrowly concerned with *appearances* and *results*. In the pursuit of slenderness, we will eat pseudo-foods, containing all manner of additives and artificial ingredients (fake fats and fake sugars), that would make our health-evangelist forebears roll over in their graves. Straining for the aerobic "burn," starving our bodies of essential nutrients, sticking fingers down our throats to "purge," stapling our stomachs, suctioning out our fat with surgical mini-vacuum cleaners: we will embrace any technique, even if it be life-threatening, just as long as it promises to make us thinner. In ways that are too literal for comfort, many of us in the United States in the 1990s would rather be dead than fat.

False Gods and Pseudo-Sins

What has happened to us? Schwartz and Seid offer brilliant historical accounts of the shifting of our cultural values toward the creation of an idol of slenderness. Beneath this shift lie a number of theological issues that are anything but trivial. The devotion of exorbitant amounts of physical, mental, emotional, and spiritual energy to the rituals of dieting seems necessary only when personal worth reduces to a matter of appearances. The preference of death to fatness can haunt us only when the meaningfulness of life itself has been seriously threatened. Thinness can become a "god" only in a context from which other more potent gods have disappeared. This, tragically, is the context in which we live.

Poised teeteringly on the scales of self-scrutiny (metaphorically if not literally), all too many of us are dangerously out of balance. Not knowing what to work for or what to worship any longer, we launch ourselves into projects of self-"perfecting," focusing on the most superficial dimensions of our identities. But even the petty "perfection" we seek is always tauntingly out of reach. Five pounds ago I thought I would be a happily satisfied woman if only I were five pounds thinner. Since beginning to write this book (a few months and a few granola binges ago), I have actually lost five pounds—without dieting, without even particularly trying. I find this baffling; I had feared that staying at home to write every day would make me put on weight. But now, instead of relaxing and rejoicing at my curious good [sic] fortune, I catch myself thinking: I would *really* be a satisfied woman if I could just lose another five pounds. . . .

Whom do I think I'm fooling? I have played this game of delaying the secularized and personalized parousia often enough by now that I really should know better. And at some levels, I suppose I do. But I am ambivalent—as I remarked in opening this chapter. On the one hand, I know that my internalized fat-phobia is a culturally conditioned phenomenon, a product of the commoditization of the human (especially the female) body by the various big money industries of cosmetics and diet, fitness and fashion. I know that it is in the best interests of a consumption-driven economy to keep me dissatisfied with my appearance so that I will continue purchasing goods and services which promise to help me toward what my culture defines as "perfection." Roberta Seid quotes the apt and insightful words of a spokesman for the beauty industry: "What we are selling is hope."[23] Indeed. Living in an uncertain world, bereft of any more compelling hopes for the cosmic—or even the immediately coming—future, many of us seem to have reduced the eschaton to a matter of appearances and individualized achievement: not everlasting beatitude, but ephemeral "beauty" becomes the goal onto which we pin our dreams. Yet, like the parousia for first-century Christians, even this paltry goal keeps receding. Here in the "between-times," we languish.

At some levels, as I said, I do know all this. But I also remain ambivalent. Because on the other hand, like so many people, I am in thrall to the "god of thinness." I do regular obeisance before him (and I say "him" advisedly; the goddesses of pre-patriarchal cultures are unabashedly huge) at the altar of my bathroom scale. I pay him daily homage through the rituals (more regular, alas, than my prayer life) of counting calories and jogging. My acute ceremonies of self-scrutiny threaten to keep me chronically out of sorts and out of kilter. A true daughter of my foremother Eve, I find it all too easy to fall prey to seductive whispers: but it is not *Sapientia* with a capital "S" that lures me; it is, rather, *sapientia* in the lower case; not ultimate Wisdom, but the fickle dictates of cultural taste. In my stubbornness, I remain staunchly "conformed to this world," when I need to be "transformed" (Rom. 12:2). What, alas, is a poor sinner to do?

This question does not allow for an easy answer; in fact, it will engage us in one way or another through most of our closing chapter. But a preliminary step toward responding to it can be taken here. One immediate thing which I—or we sinners—must do is learn how to differentiate true from false gods, and true from pseudo-sinning.

The former task sounds deceptively simple. To anyone who gave the matter serious thought, it would seem self-evident that "thinness" is a false god, too flimsy a phenomenon to bear the investment of anyone's "ultimate concern." Yet, the fact that so many of us let our sense of self-worth or our enthusiasm for living be determined by how much we weigh on a given morning reveals how blind we are to our deepest allegiances. Our real gods are not the ones (or the One) to whom we give lip service on Sundays, but the ones which attract our devotion every other day of the week. For many among us, thinness has become a mini-god. On the other hand, a true God is One who can sustain our sense of the meaningfulness of life through its inevitable tragedies, its myriad provocations to doubt and despair. No ideal of attractiveness, no goal of physical beauty, can bear this freight for very long. The "god of thinness" is no true god. We need to dethrone this idol in the dailiness of our living, to strip the false deity of dangerous powers.

But what of differentiating true from pseudo-sinning? Here, the historical materials from the previous chapter can return to serve us well. In the early centuries of the church, Christian moral theologians teach that gluttony is a sin, and they tell us why: it involves a misorientation of priorities, a failure to savor the creation and to serve the neighbor. Gluttony entails patterns of consumption that rupture the bonds of community and refuse to give due place to God. The glutton pursues immediate pleasures at the expense of other people and of other values. As an analysis of true sinning, this assessment is apt; gluttony is, indeed, a true sin.

But in the middle decades of the twentieth century, the true sin of gluttony begins to give way to a misperceived sin—the presumed "sin" of fatness. The more thinness as a cultural ideal gets linked to both beauty and health, the more synonymous with virtue it becomes. In the same manner, gluttony comes to be connected with girth, in an easy and unquestioned equation. If a person is large, it must mean s/he is a glutton. In 1954, *Life* magazine announces, with an all-too-ready moralism, "the uncompromising truth is that obesity is a result of gluttony."[24] Not so fast! Just a few years before, we were told that gluttony made us dyspeptic and dangerously thin!

The fact of the matter is that the equation between obesity and gluttony is not nearly so neat as the present "wisdom" assumes. As we shall see in the following chapter, fatness does not always issue from deranged patterns of consumption, and destructive consumption patterns do not always issue in obesity. Yet, our cultural idol of thinness has seduced us into making snap judgments about other people's behaviors, based solely on their physical appearance—and into making similarly harsh judgments about ourselves. We view fatness as if it were a moral failure, deserving of ridicule or even of condemnation. And worst of all, we seem oblivious to the destructiveness of what we are doing.

In the days of the feminist movement's emergence from the Civil Rights struggle, a popular button modified themes of racial equality, proclaiming: "It is unfair to discriminate based on the SHAPE of a person's skin." In the present arena, the slogan becomes even more apt. It reminds us that we still have a few things to learn about the difference between true and pseudo-sinning. We need to re-learn, for example, that while *gluttony* is a true sin, *girth* is not necessarily sinful at all. Equally important, we need to alert ourselves to the fact that discrimination against people on the basis of *shape* constitutes a seriously sinful behavior. In fact, this pattern of behavior lurks as a subtle snake in the grass this side of the garden of Eden. It hisses its seductions in one of the most underacknowledged prejudices of our culture—namely:

THE SIN OF WEIGHTISM

In the 1990s, in the era of "political correctness," there are few socially acceptable prejudices any more. Laws prohibit discrimination based on matters of race, sex, or national origin.

Ethnic, racist, and sexist jokes and stereotypes meet with raised eyebrows at least as often as they meet with uncritical approval (except, of course, in occasional enclaves of reaction). Since the 1960s, concerted efforts at consciousness-raising in all these areas have met with significant successes. Yet, even in this "enlightened" context, two unquestioned targets of abuse seem to remain: it continues to be permissible to "bash" gay men and lesbians, and to lambaste fat people.

These two lingering prejudices are not unrelated. In both instances, assumptions (or mis-assumptions) about morality cloud the picture. Many in our culture automatically assume homosexuality to be immoral; the current equation of thinness to beauty-health-and-virtue leads us to judge obesity in a similar fashion. Most understand the patent unfairness of victimizing another person for a matter of race, sex, or ethnicity which is an unalterable *given*; but most continue uncritically to think of sexual orientation and body size as matters of *choice* and therefore of culpability. I shall examine these assumptions more closely in beginning the next chapter. But first, it is important to understand how prevalent and pernicious the sin of weightism, in both attitudes and actions, is proving to be.

Attitudes and Actions

Prejudicial attitudes range from subtle to blatant, from simply heedless to seriously harmful. Heedless weightism pervades some of our most familiar lines of conversation: "She has such a pretty face,"[25] (meaning, the rest of her body does not conform so readily to the conventional norms of attractiveness); "He could certainly stand to lose a few pounds" (meaning, his stomach is protruding over his belt); or "She has really let herself go since the last time I saw her" (meaning, she has visibly put on some weight). Heedless weightism lurks in our popular (and judgmental) fascination with the diet "successes" and "failures" of celebrities like Elizabeth Taylor and Oprah Winfrey. Heedless weightism emerges in our unctuous condolences for weight gained and our ready compliments for weight lost. (Can we even imagine this situation the other way around? Except in the case of a very young child or the victim of a serious illness, would we ever be likely to comment admiringly, "You're really growing *plump*!" or to caution—except, perhaps, in envy—"You're getting to be so *thin*!"?) Heedless weightism suffuses the lament which I hear so often from other women and from myself: "I feel *fat* today!" when what we actually mean is that we are feeling dissatisfied with ourselves for any number of reasons. Heedless weightism occurs, in fact, anytime any of us use an adjective of body size in a pejorative rather than a merely descriptive fashion.

Such heedless thoughts and remarks can, however, culminate in serious harm. Constantly repeated, they contribute to an atmosphere of prejudice that is damaging to both emotional and physical health and well-being. Such damage begins early. In a study done in Manhattan (and subsequently replicated in other parts of the country) researchers showed children a series of pictures of other children possessing a variety of disabilities or disfigurements.[26] Experimental subjects then responded to the question, "Which of these children would you most or least like to have as your friend?" Across race, sex, economic class, and geographic area of residence in the United States, children uniformly rank the fat figure *lowest* on a scale of likability. What is perhaps most devastating about these results is that the same answer appears regardless of the body type of the child being questioned. In other words, even fat children do not want to have other fat children as friends; even fat children assume that fatness makes a person "unlikable." What does this suggest about the ways these children must be thinking and feeling about themselves?

Childhood attitudes continue and intensify in adolescence. Studies have shown that adolescent girls who are above the norms of "desirable" weight manifest symptoms of withdrawal and passivity similar to victims of various racial prejudices.[27] In comparing fat adolescents to members of other minority groups, Jean Mayer has found that fat children are not only "less happy" and "less hopeful" than their slender siblings, but also that "the improvements promised to other abused minorities are not . . . presented to [the so-called "overweight"]." While the black does not have to cease being black in order to receive civil rights, the situation is not that simple for the fat adolescent, particularly the fat young woman:

By definition, she must, before being esteemed an equal of her slender sister, cease to be her plump self. She must win a basic situation of acceptability that others . . . receive as a built-in entitlement.[28]

In other words, she cannot be valued for who she is; rather, she must change in order to become worthy of value. Once again, the presumption of alterability affects the potency of prejudice.

And prejudicial attitudes provoke prejudicial actions—for example, in education. When shown the same pictures as the children in the Manhattan study mentioned above, teachers also rate the fat child lowest in likability. Absorbing cultural attitudes that equate being fat with being "lazy" and "dumb," teachers assign lower grades to papers which are presumed to have been written by fat pupils. Fat children receive less physical affection and less after-school attention from teachers than do students who are thin.[29] A famous study by Jean Mayer and his colleagues has discerned "a strong bias in college admission against obese boys and even more against obese girls."[30] Perhaps because of prejudicial attitudes conveyed in letters of recommendation or because of interviewer bias, an obese girl is only one-third as likely as a non-obese one, with comparable entrance examination scores, to gain admission to the college of her choice. Similar biases obtain in graduate school admissions.[31]

What is true in education holds true in other areas as well. Ann Scott Beller notes that "fat army recruits can be dismissed or reassigned for cause."[32] Fat people can be denied the privilege of adopting children, simply because of weight.[33] Fat people do not have equal access to public facilities (restaurants, movie theaters, airplanes, buses, school desks, jury boxes) because of inadequate seating. Fat people are subject to medical harassment and misdiagnosis in that unrelated physical conditions tend nevertheless to be looked upon (disapprovingly) as weight-related. Troubling studies report that physicians describe their obese clients as "more weak-willed, ugly, and awkward" than other patients.[34] Insurance companies regularly deny coverage to fat people, and employers can cite difficulty in providing coverage as a rationale to mask prejudicial practices in hiring.[35] Indeed, as Sally Smith

(Executive Director of NAAFA, the National Association to Advance Fat Acceptance) summarizes the current situation:

> Myths and stereotypes are used to justify treating fat people as second-class citizens. This has a devastating effect on the quality of life for fat people. Fat people are . . . denied employment, denied promotions and raises, denied benefits, and sometimes fired, all because of their weight.[36]

What would we think if actions such as these were perpetrated against an individual because of the color—rather than the shape—of his or her skin?

Prejudicial practices in employment of fat persons have recently begun to be challenged in the courts. Flight attendants for American Airlines have filed a class action suit protesting the selectively stringent application of weight standards for company employees, claiming that such standards represent both age and sex discrimination.[37] Employees of other companies have contested weight-related firings, citing as legal warrant the prohibition against discrimination based on a physical handicap.[38] Yet, such approaches are far from ideal. If the issue is weight, why must it be couched in other terms (which then obscure the specificity of the problem of weightism)? It is a mixed benefit, at best, to classify fatness as a physical disability: on the one hand, such a classification does enable some redress against discrimination (currently, size is not a legally protected category, except in a very few states); on the other hand, however, this classification undercuts a basic goal of Size Acceptance advocates who claim that fatness does not constitute a handicap in job-performance.[39] Legal gains thus become (ironically) ideological losses.

Interlocking -isms

Even though the necessity of fighting size-discrimination in terms of other legally protected categories can serve to obscure or undercut the specific goals of the Size Acceptance movement, the stigma against weight does interconnect with a variety of other cultural -isms: classism, racism, agism, sexism, and heterosexism (to name a few). No prejudice is an island; in a world sinking deep in sin, all prejudices "shore up" one another.

Class and weight prejudices, for example. The "god of thinness" is an elitist god, and devotion to him marks a curious ritual of upward social mobility. Sociologists of Western industrialized nations have generally observed that the more affluent a society, the more slenderness connotes high social standing and fatness appears *déclassé*.[40] Certainly, such a shift in images occurs in the United States in the late nineteenth century, as girth gets downgraded from a sign of prosperity to a signal of immigrant status. In his famous work on the *Theory of the Leisure Class* published in 1899, Thorsten Veblen comments on the "delicate" and "diminutive" ideal exacted upon the wives of the wealthy.[41] Nearly a century later, his observation is borne out in demographic studies which show that women's weights vary inversely with their husband's level of income: the fatter the salary, the thinner the wife.[42] Women in high-powered careers themselves also tend to live up (or down) to a fashionably lean body standard. Indeed, according to reports from the Census Bureau and the National Center for Health Statistics, the lowest percentage of fat people in this country—both men and women—is found among the most affluent classes, whereas the highest incidence of obesity occurs in lower socioeconomic groups—most particularly, among black women living below the poverty level.[43]

Thus, issues of race (and of sex) compound the interlocking -isms of weight and class. When we as a culture sneer at fatness, we are also (wittingly or not) reflecting a set of biases about economic standing and ethnicity. In 1977, *Ebony* magazine cautions that in order to be successful, blacks will have to "leave behind the ancestral African equation of fat with wealth and health" and adopt the (white) middle class "lifestyle" of weight control.[44] Until recently, differences in ideal body image among blacks protected young black women from the disease of anorexia nervosa; but increasingly, assimilation to the dominant norms of Caucasian (thin-worshiping) culture has resulted in the cross-racial spread of this eating disorder. Indeed, in a study on "Disordered Eating in Women of Color," Maria Root suggests that:

the development of an eating disorder may . . . become a vehicle for attempting a resolution of biculturality, particularly in the face of negative racial/ethnic stereotypes that reflect a lack of appreciation of beauty that is different than the Western European ideal.[45]

The message is clear: to fit into the bastions of privilege (or at least to elude the assaults of prejudice), we must fit into smaller and smaller clothing sizes, in defiance of the ethnic morphology of our bodies—and even in defiance of their natural maturation. The cult of slenderness which amplifies class and race differences links to a cult of youthfulness as well. To grow heavier—to thicken in the waistline, to convert a portion of muscle tissue to fat—is a normal part of the process of aging. The drive for perpetual thinness opposes this process. As Cheryl Ritenbaugh remarks, "thinness as a culturally valued commodity is related to the value placed on youth."[46] She calls our attention to the fact that the tabulated weight-to-height standards for all adults are based on the data for 25-year-olds. (Indeed, tables such as that developed by the Metropolitan Life Insurance Company disclose not only age bias, but an element of ethnic bias as well, since they compute as "ideal" the body type of the long and lanky American of northern European ancestry rather than the more stolid build of southern or eastern European—not to mention African—extraction.[47]) Roberta Seid laments our efforts to create a "uni-age society"—a society in which we all struggle to preserve or recover the shape we had fresh out high school or college. She sees this battle—aptly—as evidence of our desire for control over nature, our resistance to the ineluctable processes of decay. Agists as well as weightists in our joint veneration of slenderness and of youth, we react harshly toward those whose sags and softnesses remind us that our bodies are mortal.[48]

In our patriarchal culture, such harshness indisputably targets women more fiercely than men. Sexism and weightism interlock so tightly that imagining one apart from the other seems well-nigh impossible. Can we imagine a world in which women are not preoccupied with dieting; in which women actually like our bodies; in which women do not compose 90% of those victimized by disorders like anorexia and bulimia and compulsive eating; in which, in fact, such disorders simply disappear because no one feels the urge to obsess over eating and not eating in pursuit of an unrealistic shape, and no one feels impelled to seek self-definition through the competitive games of "skinnier than thou"? Can we imagine a world in which women receive sufficient sustenance from our vocations and our relationships that we do not find ourselves turning to food for consolation? Can we imagine a world in which it is permissible for a woman to take up space—to be big and bold and powerful, to be a Maltese goddess—without anyone's feeling a threatened urge to pare her down to size? Can we imagine a world in which eating is an unambivalent feast at the breast of the Mother, a world in which the roundness of our female bodies bespeaks the round of birth and death in ways that comfort rather than terrify? To borrow a potent phrase from Monique Wittig: Can we even imagine such a world—or failing that, invent?[49]

In the world in which we live, this side of Malta and this side of the Garden of Eden, heterosexism works in tandem with sexism in shoring up prejudices against fatness. Women's pursuit of thinness is keenly prompted by the urge to appear desirable to men (and the higher the man's status, the thinner the woman must be); women's denial of appetite and size and power and self-nurture is primarily practiced for the benefit of men. Clinical psychologist Laura Brown reports on research showing that "internalized fat-oppressive attitudes are more present in persons of *either* gender who want to be found attractive by men, while they occur at lower rates in persons of either gender who wish to be found attractive by women."[50] As a group, lesbians are relatively freer of eating disorders than other women (gay males, alas, are relatively more afflicted).

Prejudices against fatness parallel prejudices against homosexuality in a number of arenas. Both fat people and homosexuals are seen as refusing (willfully) to conform to the norms of the dominant culture—whether these norms be constituted as "family" or as "fitness" values (as if gay men and lesbians never participated in committed, familial relationships; as if fat people never participated in exercise programs). Both gayness and fatness function to blur traditional gender distinctions, thereby upsetting the order of a society which continues to be conveniently bifurcated into male and female spheres. Gay men and lesbians threaten these gender distinctions by not fitting norms of "masculinity" and "femininity" in such diverse areas as dress, gesture, voice and inflection, and sex/gender roles. Fat people threaten gender distinctions in perhaps more subtle ways: fatness tends to blur or to "cross" gender characteristics (fat women, because of their size, can appear "mannish"; fat men, because of deposits of body fat, can look "feminized"); fat women in particular do not "fit" the diminutive norm which is demanded of women in order that we be seen as desirable, sexual beings.[51]

Further, both fatness and gayness force us to confront the issue of *appetite* in ways that can be very uncomfortable for our lingering Puritanism. Popular prejudice associates homosexuality with promiscuity—not because gay men and lesbians are any more inclined to promiscuous behavior than heterosexuals, but rather because gay men and lesbians undeniably engage in sexual activity for the purpose of *pleasure* rather than for any presumed intent of procreation. Likewise, popular prejudice associates fatness with indulgent consumption—even though many studies report that fat people actually do not eat more than others do.[52] Consequently, when we view a person who is fat, we are all too quick to project onto that person our own ambivalence about matters of pleasure and appetite. Terrified by the insatiable hungers in ourselves, proud yet angry over the amount of energy we devote to self-restraint, we read into fatness an intolerable image of lost control. Marianne Ware captures this dynamic pointedly in her poem, "To those who use 'fat' as a definitive adjective": "And what is 'fat' to you: /.... / perhaps your own voraciousness—/ projected?"[53] Corseted by our Puritan heritage, our ethic of eating remains a restrictive one, filled with "Thou shalt not's" and lauding abstemiousness as a mark of election (Gregory's admonitions to the contrary notwithstanding). As with sex, so with food: we have failed to develop an ethic of responsible sensuous enjoyment. The fat (or gay) person bears the brunt of our bad conscience and of our moral failure.

Like heterosexism (and so many other -isms as well), weightism functions in a territory where personal issues become political, and issues of legal rights take root in language. How much a person weighs (like what manner of sexual orientation s/he embraces) may appear to be an intimately personal matter. And to an extent, this assessment is apt. So, a significant step forward occurs when anyone moves from overt gay- or fat-bashing to the "liberal," let-live attitude of "whatever people like that choose to do to their bodies in the privacy of their own homes is their own business (as long as my son or daughter doesn't get involved)." But simply espousing the right to privacy is not enough. Being fat *is* a personal matter, but it is not merely a personal matter. As long as discriminatory acts and attitudes are in force (in education, employment, health care, insurance, and access to public facilities), fatness is also a political issue. As long as "thin privilege" exists—the privilege that automatically confers preferential treatment upon certain students, employees, patients, clients, and customers, simply because of their more "acceptable" body size— fatness is a political issue. As long as poorly regulated (at best, ineffectual; at worst, health-endangering) weight-loss industries continue to feed off the culturally-enforced insecurity of people whose body shapes are considered "*un*acceptable," fatness is a political issue.[54]

And political issues invariably take root in language. Three decades ago, when racism and sexism were first moving to the forefront of political awareness, proponents of equal rights began calling attention to the ways in which linguistic images and omissions served to buttress oppression. Slogans of "Black is Beautiful"; shifts in terminology from "colored" to Negro to Black to African-American; crusades to translate from so-called "generic" to genuinely gender-inclusive language; campaigns to reclaim the positive potency of words rendered "ugly" by cultural lip-curling ("witch," "hag," "dyke"—and now even "feminist"): all of these efforts point to the importance of language in the press toward liberation.

Language is similarly important for the Size Acceptance movement. Reclaiming the adjective "fat" as descriptive rather pejorative is a key issue. Currently, as activists and advocates note, the term has considerable "flinch value."[55] It is a wounding word. We apply it viciously to ourselves (I feel so *fat*! I would rather be dead than fat!). We use it viciously of other people (children's taunts of "fatty, fatty, two-by-four" are particularly cruel, though adults' derisive comments can betray equal cruelty beneath a more subtle veneer). Marianne Ware's poem, again, speaks volumes:

> . . . what's couched, malevolently,
> behind those meager letters:
> one vowel, two consonants,
> as in "old" and "Jew."[56]

Or if we do not use the word "fat" judgmentally, we avoid it altogether. We seek well-intentioned euphemisms (plump, heavy, large), or we attempt a more clinical vocabulary (obese, overweight). The problem with these euphemisms is the problem with all euphemisms: apart from being imprecise and misleading, they paradoxically exaggerate the taboo surrounding the notion they are attempting to "prettify." The problem with the clinical terms is that they medicalize the matter of body size, conveying the assumption that fatness is inherently pathological. Besides which, as mentioned before in conjunction with the Metropolitan Life Insurance Tables, the concept of "overweight" presupposes a "normal" or normative weight which one can be *over*. In contrast, Laura Brown reminds us: "'Fat' is a descriptive term which, stripped of its cultural baggage, has no necessary implications of wrongness or deviation (imagine for a minute the parallel terms: 'undermale' as the equivalent of 'female,' for instance)."[57]

In a society sensitized to issues of racial equality, we would certainly not refer to an African-American person as "underwhite"! The Size Acceptance Movement (championed by groups such as NAAFA: the National Association to Advance Fat Acceptance [founded in 1971 as the National Association to Aid Fat Americans]) insists that fatness is simply a variant on the continuum of body sizes—just as blackness or brownness are variants on the spectrum of racial colorations. There are those who contest this analogy: who insist that race is an invariant *given* whereas weight can be altered and controlled; who maintain that race is not a matter of pathology whereas excessive [*sic*] weight constitutes a health risk. We shall examine these arguments more closely in the following chapter. For now, however, the more crucial question remains: *even if* the opponents of Fat Liberation are right, are they—are we, am I—justified in *stigmatizing* fatness (that of other people, that of our own bodies)? Is weightism a pseudo-ism, simply one more item on the ever-expanding liberal "political correctness" agenda? Or does weightism rather constitute a serious sin—in fact, a sin:

Against Neighbor, Against God, and Against Me

"Sin" is a sharp word, a strong word; yet, I find it a sadly appropriate word to describe weightist actions and attitudes from the vantage point of Christian moral theology. It seems to me not only petty but hateful to sneer at another human being for his or her body shape—or for any other reason. It seems both wrong-headed and hurtful to make judgments about others based solely on appearances—whether such judgments assume a facile equation between fatness and gluttony, or fatness and incompetence, or fatness and "unlikability." It seems "small-minded" and "narrow-minded" (both puns polemically intended) to force conformity to a single standard of social acceptability, neglecting the diversity of the creation and the changeability of our cultural norms of beauty. It is prideful and deceitful to project the distrust we have of our own bodies and appetites onto others whom we outcaste as less "disciplined" than we. Perhaps worst of all, it is dangerous and destructive to harass another person into weight-loss preoccupations and/or procedures which can ultimately be life-threatening. If sin lies in any act that violates the love of neighbor, then weightism manifests a painful example of sinfulness.

Nor is it simply love of neighbor which is at issue in weightist actions and attitudes; love of God is also at stake. Any act of judgmentalism opposes the God who stands as sole Judge over human living. Any hatred contravenes a God who is loving-kindness. Any act of scorn defies the God who is mercy and amazing grace. Any narrow-minded conformity runs counter to a God who is abundance and generosity. Any elevation of a superficial attribute, such as thinness, into pseudo-divine status is an offense against the God who alone is God, and alone is worthy of worship.

Finally, weightism is also a sin against self—a sin against me. A few years ago, a wire report from Memphis, Tennessee, carried the story of a man who tried to have his wife killed (on Mother's Day, no less!) "for failing to lose weight after she had a baby."[58] Admittedly, the example is extreme. But there are (alas) tragic analogies between the brutality of wanting another person killed because of her weight, and wishing myself dead for the identical reason. To sob that I would rather be dead than fat is not simply to voice an innocent lament; it is to utter a remark that carries serious consequences. It affects the ways I relate to other people (condescendingly, if they are fatter than I; enviously, if they are thinner). It affects the ways I relate to my Creator and my Ultimate Context (with resentment and rejection rather than gratitude and celebration). And it affects the ways I relate to myself: harshly, punitively, despairingly. Of what are the self-tortures of eating disorders born if not of internalized weightism, of introjected disgust at fatness? How often, in a shocking moment of clarity, in the middle of a binge or a purge—a moment when my heart was pounding and I could feel myself sweating, trembling, weeping, aching, gasping for breath, clutching for control—how often have I felt the idea sear through me: "I'm killing myself. What I am doing is committing a slow form of suicide!"?

There is no virtue in the pursuit of thinness if it proceeds by such self-destructive means. Indeed, quite the opposite. To hate my body—whatever its weight or shape—is to despise a gift from my Creator. It is to reveal my tragic distance from Eden: my shame at embodiedness; my attempts at hiding. It is to lay down a living sacrifice, at the foot of a horribly false altar. It is simultaneously to break the first, the second, and the sixth commandments. To return to that sharp, strong, and sadly appropriate word, it is to sin.

Like most sins, however, weightism is one for which I both can and cannot be fairly held accountable. It is a set of acts which I culpably commit, yet it is also a state which I seem almost inevitably "born into." A patriarchal, consumerist culture has taught the profitable "thinness" ideal so well that much of the time I do not even recognize how thoroughly I have been conditioned. Twenty years ago, I scarcely heard the hurtful silences of exclusive language. Today, I am only beginning to tune my ear to the fat-phobic undertones of thoughtless remarks about body size. Breaking free of prevailing assumptions and stereotypes is difficult: particularly when I have barely taken the first step of recognizing that they are, in fact, merely *assumptions*; particularly when the principalities and powers of vested interests are hard at work to keep me in ignorance. I *am* guilty of the sin of weightism—directed at others as well as at myself. But in part, my guilt comes from the innocence of having naively appropriated the ideals which my culture professes. I *am* "conformed to this age"—but so naturally and artlessly so, that much of the time, it does not even appear to be conformity.

Since, however, it is Christian teaching which cautions against such "conforming" and extols the countering wisdom of transformation (all the while heralding a message of goodwill to *all* people), it would seem logical to expect the church to stand in the forefront of opposition to the hateful prejudices of our cultural -isms. Particularly in the case of weightism: Christians should surely be among the first to see through the vanity of worldly concerns about physical appearance! But the contrary is more often the case. Since the 1950s, a Christian weight-loss industry has been flourishing, feeding off the facile conflation of fat and sin (and forgetting that the traditional teachings of the church condemn consumptive behaviors but say nothing about cosmetic matters of body shape and size). Charles Shedd's *Pray Your Weight Away* (1957) sets the trend in motion, followed by Prayer-Diet Clubs, and the Jesus System for Weight Control. The 1970s continue with Overeaters Victorious and such graphic titles as *More of Jesus and Less of Me* (1976) and *Help Lord—the Devil Wants Me Fat!* (1978). In his 1988 volume *Thin, Trim, and Triumphant: How to Get God's Help in Losing Unwanted Pounds*, pastor Roger Campbell voices the typical and ardent claim: "If God cares about the appearance of lilies that are seen for a few weeks and then wither and die, my appearance must be important to Him."[59]

Hasn't something gone amiss in this interpretation? As I read the passage from Jesus' discourses to which Campbell is alluding, I hear a very different message. The text proclaims:

> Therefore I tell you, do not be anxious . . . about your body, what
> you shall put on. Is not . . . the body more than clothing? . . .
> Consider the lilies of the field. . . . (Matthew 6:25, 28; Luke 12:22,
> 27)

Rather than highlighting the importance of appearance by elevating it to a divine concern, the gospel text seems to me to do just the opposite: to undercut our persistent preoccupation with what clothing we wear, what size we are, how "attractive" we appear. To disagree with Campbell is not, however, to engage in some gnostic ploy of discounting the body. Bodies *do* matter. Health and wholeness and stewardship matter. Feeling gracefully attuned to the flesh, because it is the generous gift of our Creator, matters. But physical appearance does not—particularly not when it is made to conform to some culturally defined and distorted equation of beauty = thinness (= virtue, = a mini-god).

In the same text to which Campbell makes reference above, Jesus exhorts:

> Do not be anxious about your life, what you shall eat or what you
> shall drink. . . . Is not life more than food?

Indeed! But I must confess from long personal experience that I know of no better way to make myself anxious about what I shall eat and to elevate food all out of proportion in my life than to embark upon some weight-loss dieting ritual exacted by the god of thinness! A balanced Christian theology of food and diet, therefore, requires not so much that I work to lose weight as that I work to gain a sense of what truly matters: that I learn to differentiate true from false gods and true from pseudo-sinning; that I learn to focus appropriately on actions and attitudes, letting resultant appearances take care of themselves. Thinness is a false god. Fatness is a pseudo-sin. On the other hand, however, the vicious attitudes of weightism and the voracious acts of gluttony are true sins—hurtful violations of the law of love for self, neighbor, Creator, and creation. Whether or not I can help the eventual size and shape of my body, I can certainly help the ways in which I respond toward myself and toward my fellow creatures. Whether or not I can help my eventual weight, I *can* help the ways in which I respond to the pleasures and perils of appetite. At least, as a good Presbyterian, I trust that I can help such things *by the grace of God!* In the next chapter, I shall examine more closely *how*.

♦   ♦   ♦

The forbidden fruit of which Eve partook never promised to make her thin or beautiful. It did, however, promise to make her wise. Seeking to sort true from pseudo-evil and appropriate from inappropriate accountability, I, too, want a taste of that wisdom. But having learned something from the tragic story of my fore-mother, I know that a taste can be dangerous without the grace to assimilate and apply it well. And so, a daughter of Eve, I stretch out my hand . . . not toward the forbidden fruit at the center of Eden, but rather toward the sapiential fruits of the Spirit.

Fruits of the Spirit

"WHENEVER YOU SEE A FAT CHRISTIAN"

I reach out my hand, and immediately I am slapped back . . . by remarks such as the following: "Whenever you see a fat Christian, you're looking at one who is not walking with the Lord."[1] Although I do not qualify as fat by any reasonable definition of the term (but when in the recent past have any of us—women in particular—been able to define that adjective reasonably?), I still feel stung by the sharpness of such a statement.[2] I find myself pondering retorts along the lines of: "Whenever you hear a judgmental Christian . . . " I picture in my mind that wryly comic biblical image (which so puzzled and intrigued me as a child) of people with logs sticking out of their eyes, eagerly attempting to extract specks from the eyes of their neighbors.I hear echoes of warnings about bearing false witness and casting first stones. But then I remind myself that the fruits of the Spirit for which I am hungering are reputed to include patience and gentleness and self-control. So I back away from my stung and stinging responses.

Let me try again—this time, by way of counterquestioning rather than counterattack. Is it true, as the preceding citation would have it, that fatness indicates sinful disobedience? I have been insisting otherwise throughout this book, insisting that *gluttony* and *weightism* are manifestations of sin, but that fatness itself is morally neutral. While scripture condemns "making a god of the belly" by elevating the pleasures of food above devotion to God, it says nothing in specific about corpulence. While early Christian moral theologians decry both excessive indulgence and excessive abstinence, they remain largely silent on the matter of body size. In fact, a variety of texts from the medieval era up through the first decades of the twentieth century associate glut-tony with indigestion and emaciation rather than with fatness. For generations with assumptions and biases different from our own, it is considered quite possible to be a "thin glutton," or to be a *stoutly* obedient Christian.

Of course, in the latter decades of the twentieth century, we do have access to a wealth of scientific information about nutri-tion and health and "stoutness" which was not available to earlier generations. So the matter of the relationship between girth and gluttony has now entered into the medical, as well as the moral arena. Given contemporary insights, it becomes all the more important to reconsider specific questions of the linkages be-tween overeating and so-called "overweight," between physical size and physical health, and between fatness and destructive behaviors related to food. In considering these linkages (or miss-ing linkages), my interests are both personal and pastoral. I want to know *how much* those of us who have problems with food and fatness can fairly be expected to help our situations; and I want to know *how* we can best help ourselves (and one another) toward recovery.

HOW MUCH CAN WE HELP?

Overeating and Overweight: Is Fatness Culpable?

From the pronouncement in a 1954 issue of *Life* magazine, cited in the previous chapter ("The uncompromising truth is that obesity is a result of gluttony"), to the one cited at the opening of this chapter ("Whenever you see a fat Christian . . . "), popular wisdom in the United States over the past few decades has insisted on the "common sense" equation that "too much" weight comes from eating "too much" food. There is a certain compelling force to this reasoning. It rests on one of our favored assumptions since the scientific revolution—that the human body is a machine, operating on a uniform and quantifiable model of so-much-in equals so-much-out. Further, both the equation and its mechanistic presuppositions offer us comforting illusions of Deuteronomic justice ("a pound for a pound") and of mathematical control. Those who weigh more must eat more; to weigh less, we must simply eat less. The matter is allegedly that "uncompromising" and plain.

But is it? We cling so tenaciously to our mechanistic paradigm that even in the face of repeated personal failures to lose weight in a lasting fashion by merely eating less food, we are more inclined to blame ourselves than our presumptive model. "I've been eating only 1200 calories a day for a week," we cry—or, in the equally familiar moralized version of the lament, "I've been being so *good*—and I've still gained a pound. What's wrong with me?" Now I do know, as a theologian, that we are all sinners, and I do know as a recovering compulsive weight-watcher that dieting makes cheaters of us all. . . . But even given the pervasiveness of human fallenness and foibles, I also know that there is something suspicious about a paradigm of weight control that works as it is "supposed to" less than 10% of the time. So I feel compelled to begin challenging the popular wisdom of that "common sense" equation.

Hearteningly, I am not alone in doing so. An increasing body of scientific literature suggests that fatness is not a simple, mechanistic matter of over-fueling the body, but that it involves a far more complex set of variables—variables like heredity and "set-point" and metabolic "efficiency" and evolutionary adaptation. There was a time in the early days of our species when an unpredictable food supply made "survival of the fattest" the rule; some of our bodies have not yet forgotten!

Because the point seems counterintuitive, or at least runs counter to the popular prejudices we have held for so long, it cannot be stated too often: fat people do not necessarily eat more food than those who are thin. Listen to the words of an expert— Wayne Wooley, Co-Director of the Eating Disorders Clinic of the

121

Department of Psychiatry, University of Cincinnati College of Medicine:

> All available evidence suggests that there is nothing "abnormal" about the way fat people eat. Some are big eaters, some are not; and the same is true of thin people. . . . Fat people don't eat faster, they don't snack more often, and they don't eat more sweets and other carbohydrates than non-fat people.[3]

A study on "Eating Habits of Obese and Normal Weight Humans" published in the *International Journal of Obesity* concurs that "Fat people cannot consistently be demonstrated to eat more or differently than thin people."[4] In an article which dares to pose the radical question, "Should Obesity Be Treated at All?," eating disorders specialist Susan Wooley joins forces with Wayne Wooley to conclude: "Although occasional studies have found overeating by the obese, the majority have found no difference in the food intakes of obese and lean infants, children, adolescents, and adults."[5]

But if overeating is not the distinguishing cause and feature of fatness, then what is? Rather than a single mathematical equation, a variety of factors contribute to a composite answer. Heredity is primary among them. In a landmark study conducted in Denmark in 1986 (and replicated in Sweden in 1990), University of Pennsylvania psychiatrist Albert Stunkard discovered that adopted children more closely resemble their biological parents than their adoptive parents in body weight.[6] In a study comparing identical twins, other siblings, and persons not related by blood, Claude Bouchard of Laval University in Quebec has demonstrated that the tendency to gain weight in response to consuming excess calories follows familial patterns.[7] Still other studies suggest that there is an inherited dimension to metabolism and to the propensity of fat cells either to break down fat or to absorb and store it.[8]

All of these studies indicate that nature, and not simply nurture (or overnurture), plays an important part in determining that some among us will be fatter than others. In fact, it is probable that weight, like other physical traits, is normally distributed across the human population in a bell-shaped (or more suitably, pear-shaped?) curve.[9] Even if all the children in Lake

Wobegon can genuinely be "above average," it is still not possible for all of us in the United States to be "below average" when it comes to the biological distribution of body sizes.

Still, it is no more appropriate to suggest a simple genetic explanation for weight than it is to propose a straightforward and simplistic behavioral one. Rather, the most helpful models are interactive, disclosing the interdependence of inherited predispositions, environmental influences, and individual responses. All of these factors combine in the phenomenon known as the "set-point." Set-point theory, first proposed in 1972 and popularized a decade later by William Bennett and Joel Gurin in *The Dieter's Dilemma*, hypothesizes that every human body has a weight level which it maintains naturally, without extraordinary measures of diet and exercise, and which it works to defend against extreme changes in either direction.[10] Research by Allen Sims in the early 1970s found that "normal" weight subjects have as much difficulty gaining weight and maintaining extra pounds as the "overweight" traditionally have in achieving and maintaining a loss.[11] Working to stay within its accustomed homeostatic range, each body adjusts its basal metabolism to adapt to the amount of food it receives. A low calorie diet thus prompts a general metabolic "slow down," during which the body learns to subsist on fewer calories than it needed before. Hence, the all-too-familiar phenomenon of the weight-loss plateau: the frustrated dieter is still eating as little as during her first jubilantly successful weeks, but the number on her scales refuses to budge; the body (with a primal, evolutionary memory of food shortages) has made itself more calorie-efficient in order to withstand its period of enforced starvation. And hence, also, the even more frustrating (and well-nigh inevitable) phenomenon of weight gain following a calorie-restricted diet. Until the body returns, slowly, to its pre-starvation metabolic rate (and depending on the frequency and duration of dieting, it may never make it all the way back again), it simply needs fewer calories for fuel: so it eagerly stores its new excess as fat—stocking up, as it were, for the next unpredictable famine.

The phenomenon of the set-point, however, does not exist in a vacuum. While a certain homeostatic weight range is a biological given for every human body, environmental and behavioral factors also interact to modify this range. If șuch were not the case, statistics cited in the previous chapter on the relationship between class and weight would not make sense. Two common phenomena of contemporary U.S. culture contribute to the general elevation of set-point weights: a diet high in fats and refined carbohydrates, and a sedentary life-style. These factors affect all of us to varying degrees, but in particular they help to account for the correlation between lower incomes and higher weights in our society. What foods can a family living below the poverty level afford to buy? How much regular aerobic exercise can a single parent get when she must meet the demands of home and child care on top of a full-time job? While it is true that genetic inheritance and biological set-point do not exclusively and unalterably predetermine weight, to tell a poor African-American woman (the U.S. population with the highest incidence of "obesity") that she is "free" to shed pounds and shift her set-point downwards may be about as realistic as to tell her she is "free" to get rich and to get leisure time.

A third environmental and behavioral factor which ironically contributes to the alteration of biological set-points is that of repeated "yo yo" dieting. After each diet, as we have just seen, the body attempts to return to its accustomed pre-diet weight. It does so not only by converting calories to energy with greater (starvation-induced) metabolic efficiency, leaving more "excess" calories to be stored as fat. It also does so by seeking to refill its fat cells before any other body tissues are rebuilt. While the body loses both fat and muscle on a weight-loss diet, in its urgent re-building program, it is mostly fat which is regained. This phenomenon has been scientifically analysed as the result of unusually high levels of lipoprotein lipase (an enzyme that promotes fat-storage) circulating in the blood from the time of a diet until the time when pre-diet fat levels are restored.[12] Virtually every excess post-diet calorie goes to fat: and when recent deprivation has made the circulating enzyme levels sufficiently high and the metabolic rate sufficiently low, as few as 800 excess calories can result in the gain of a pound! (So much for the uniform "body-machine" equation of one pound everywhere and always equals 3500 excess calories.)[13] Furthermore, every pound re-gained after a calorie-restricted diet works to alter the fat-to-lean ratio of the body in the direction of greater fat . . . which means an even greater metabolic "efficiency" (since fat burns fewer calories than muscle) and an even higher set-point.

The news seems grim, but it is not without its important lessons. The first among them consists of a response to our title question: "Is fatness culpable?" In view of the evidence, we must answer with a qualified negative: fat is not any more culpable than something like socioeconomic status is culpable. The analogy is far from perfect, but it is illuminating: while rigorous adherence to a work ethic or a diet ethic *can* serve to alter existing conditions of class or of weight, such an ethic never operates completely unconstrained (by factors such as unequal educational and occupational opportunities in the wider economy, or unequal metabolic rates in the "economy" of the individual body). If all poverty were produced by extravagant spending on the part of the poor, or all fatness were produced by voracious overeating, then culpability would be a more appropriate category. But as we have seen in the instance of fatness, such an analysis does not hold true to the data. When a genetic predisposition to be at the upper end of the weight curve combines with a metabolism rendered ever-more-efficient by frequent bouts of dieting, such that the maximum number of calories one can consume daily and not *gain* weight is 1700 (and 1600 calories daily was characterized as "semistarvation" rations by the Dutch authorities during German occupation of the Netherlands); when fat cells emptied and re-emptied by yo-yo diets cry out constantly to be re-filled, and high levels of lipoprotein lipase enzymes circulate through the bloodstream, ever eager to perform the task . . . when we are aware that such conditions prevail in the bodies of our fat brothers and sisters, we can scarcely look upon them simple-mindedly and moralistically as guilty gluttons (or disobedient Christians) any more.[14] Rather, we should be moved to consider the question raised by Dr. Jean Mayer of the Harvard School of Public Health: "Is it not conceivable that [fat people]—the too easily and too frequently condemned—are, in terms of the urgent appetites which drive them, heroes of rigorous self-mastery?"[15]

There is a second vital lesson to be learned from the grim data about the relative intractability and non-culpability of fatness. It is a lesson of the need for us as a culture—fat and non-fat persons alike—to reorient our ideals and our aspirations. As long as we worship the god of thinness, stigmatizing and discriminating against people (including ourselves) because of body size, we paradoxically create a situation of ever-increasing fatness. When we create pressures to diet in order to conform to a cultural demand for slenderness, we set in motion the self-defeating physiological cycles of lowered metabolisms and elevated set-points. Equally destructively, we activate the psychological cycles of perfectionism and self-loathing which result in disordered eating (episodic starving compensated by bingeing and purging, in a painfully destructive spiral).

We need, I repeat, to reorient our aspirations. Rather than prizing thinness at all costs (prizing it so much that we would rather be dead than fat—sometimes, all too literally so), we must learn to prize *not* thinness, but health: healthful patterns of eating and exercising, healthful patterns of attending to the bodies which have been entrusted to our care. The appropriate orientation for those who would be "transformed rather than conformed" is toward actions and attitudes, not appearances. If we are savoring and not devouring the goods of the earth; if we are stewarding and not subjugating our bodies; if we are cherishing and not despising the variety of shapes in which human beings come to be configured, then we are in harmony with the deeper ideals and aspirations of Christianity. Indeed, looked at from the perspective of Christian theology, the goal of losing weight in and for itself is more than a little like the goal of reaching heaven: *not* because being thin would be "heavenly" (It wouldn't; it isn't; stop thinking that way!), but because the focus on such an outcome misses the more important point. We are to do justice and love mercy *not* for the purpose of winning an eternal reward, but for the sole and sufficient reason that a life led in love with God is intrinsically valuable. We are to eat healthfully and exercise appropriately not for the purpose of winning an improbable place in the lower 10% of the weight distribution curve, but rather for the more sustaining reason that a life lived in vigor and in sensuous responsibility is intrinsically rewarding.

Physical Size and Physical Health: Is Fatness Bad Stewardship?

Having granted that "overweight" does not necessarily imply overeating, that fatness has as much to do with genetic inheritance and the dynamics of set-point as it does with patterns of food consumption, and that low calorie diets fail for physiological (and not simply motivational) reasons roughly 90% of the time, one might still want to argue that there is more than cosmetic significance to committing oneself to the ever-vigilant effort to be among the few who win lasting results in the weight-loss battle. After all, if we are to prize health and to practice stewardship, then are we not obliged to fight fatness, with whatever measures necessary? Devotees of the cult of slender fitness have been at work since the 1950s to convince us that the fat person is not only "unattractive," but also unhealthy. Is this true? Does fatness betray bad stewardship of our God-given bodies?

More and more, the popular equation of fatness and ill health is being called into question as much as the "common sense" equation of overeating and overweight. An outstanding emblem of this new questioning is the fact that the Metropolitan Life Insurance Company, responsible for bringing the national "epidemic" of obesity before the American Medical Association in 1951, revised its height/weight tables *upwards* in 1983.[16] These revisions were made in the light of a variety of studies which not only failed to replicate Louis Dublin's earlier finding that lower weights improved life expectancy, but actually showed greater health and longevity for people whose weights were *above* the stated MLIC standards. For example:

(1) From 1952–1957, Lester Breslow, Consultant to the President's Commission on the Health Needs of the Nation, studied San Francisco longshoremen, for whom the average weight was 17% above the MLIC figures. His expected discovery of increased mortality tied to weight was confounded by the datum that these "overweight" men in fact manifested a "strikingly lower incidence

of coronary and other mortality" than all other compared samples of California males.

(2) Between 1950 and 1979, researchers Paul Sorlie, Tavia Gordon, and William Kannel conducted "The Framingham Study," a longitudinal investigation of over 5000 men and women. The Framingham results indicated that for men, the greatest longevity correlated with weights 25%–40% above the current MLIC figures, and the shortest life spans were experienced by the thinnest members of the population. For women, slightly higher mortality rates were the case for either the very fat or the very thin, but no significant correlation between size and shortened life span pertained for the vast numbers in the middle weight ranges.

(3) In 1980, Ancel Keys published the findings of a twenty-five year "multivariate analysis of death and coronary heart disease" in seven countries. On the basis of his data, he announced, "The idea has been greatly oversold that the risk of dying prematurely or of having a heart attack is directly related to relative body weight," and concluded that better longevity actually correlates with average or slightly above average weight. Further, in a review of thirteen studies on obesity and mortality, Keys discovered—like the Framingham researchers—that weight has no significant impact on health for the middle 80% of women, but that it contributes to a health risk only for the heaviest 10% and the thinnest 10%.

(4) In 1983, the *American Journal of Public Health* reviewed the literature on the relationship of overweight to heart disease, diabetes, hypertension, cholesterol, and overall premature mortality, and found that while "severe" overweight is associated with decreased longevity, *moderate* overweight is "not . . . an important risk factor."

(5) In 1985, Reubin Andres, Clinical Director of the National Institute on Aging of the National Institutes of Health, assessed the accumulating volume of studies on weight and mortality, and concurred with the conclusion that a significant risk of early death occurs only at the weight extremes of a population, with extremes in the direction of excessive thinness being as dangerous as excessive fat.

(6) In 1988, psychologist Eva Szekely reported on data demonstrating that "women between 5' 3" and 5' 6" weighing between 115 and 194 pounds are equally healthy on average," and confirmed that "being underweight is as much a health risk as being overweight, [and] . . . in terms of health what matters most is having a stable weight."[17]

What we discover in this rapid survey of the scientific literature is that the presumed equation of fatness with poor health has far more to do with prejudice than with fact. Even the readily assumed connection between high weight and high blood pressure reveals methodological flaws, if not outright bias. The correlation, where it exists, can just as easily (and even more accurately) be attributed to the fact that the fat populations traditionally studied comprise individuals who have subjected their bodies to frequent and damaging yo-yo diets and who have been subjected by their culture to the chronic stress of stigmatization. No wonder blood pressures soar! As Vivian Mayer points out:

> the handful of studies existing on non-persecuted fat people suggests that they are quite healthy, whereas studies of persecuted groups other than fat people, such as black people, show these groups to suffer from many of the diseases "characteristic" of fat people.[18]

Where studies do disclose health risks attendant upon fatness, they show only correlation, not causation: that is to say, just because fatness coexists with a particular condition does not mean that the fat has caused it. Rather, the causes are more clearly discerned in further phenomena also linked with being fat in our thin-worshiping society: overstress (as Mayer suggests), overdieting, and underexercise.

Dieting does, indeed, constitute a serious health hazard—far more serious than fatness, according to many authorities. Apart from the metabolic havoc and the escalation of fat deposition which we have already discussed, dieting has been shown to cause atherosclerosis in laboratory rats, to increase their risk of heart attack and stroke, to destroy significant levels of bodily protein, and to lead to episodes of compulsive eating.[19] In humans, the last-named outcome becomes particularly acute. Psychological studies with so-called "restrained" eaters—that is, with those of us who are constantly monitoring our caloric intake, trying vigilantly to keep ourselves on one diet or another—show that they (or we) are far more disposed than simple "unrestrained" eaters to engage in "negative affect eating": to binge in response to stress or anxiety.[20] In other words, the compulsive dieting triggers compulsive eating, rather than the other way around. Restraint, rather than the lack of it, paradoxically turns us into gluttons, with all the dangerous consequences for our spiritual as well as our physical well-being.

Beyond overdieting, yo-yoing back and forth between purges and binges, *underexercising* represents a serious health risk associated with so-called "overweight." Many factors keep fat people from exercising appropriately: inaccessible equipment and facilities, fear of ridicule, disheartening and self-defeating goals which focus obsessively on getting thin rather than on getting healthy. Ironically, the popular conflation of fatness with unhealthiness works to exaggerate a sense of susceptibility to illness or injury, thereby discouraging fat people from the very activity which would give them the greatest health benefits.[21] George Blackburn of Harvard Medical School notes that a tendency toward diabetes and high blood pressure can often be corrected by a very moderate reduction of weight, lost by exercise alone rather than through participation in a calorie-restricted diet.[22] William Bennett, editor of the Harvard Medical School Health Letter, agrees. Diabetes and high blood pressure improve from regular exercise, he affirms, "*even when no weight is lost.*" Further, he notes, exercise improves the aerobic capacity of the heart, training it to work efficiently in response to exertion and protecting it from "the hazards of unexpectedly high loads."[23] Failure to participate in aerobic exercise tailored to the specific needs and capabilities of our individual bodies does indeed exemplify bad stewardship. (For that matter, so does compulsive *over*exercising, stressing the body beyond its needs for rest as well as for exertion.) Failure to get skinny as a result of exercising appropriately, however, is not a stewardship issue at all. It is simply a fact of life, a manifestation of the rich variety of healthful shapes and sizes that our bodies are intended to be.

Fatness and Food/Diet Addictions: Are We Helpless?

I have been arguing for the past several pages that our priorities are out of order: that we as a culture keep expending vast amounts of time, energy, and money in the pursuit of thinness, justifying this pursuit to ourselves (when we even stop to think that it might need justifying) as a matter of appropriate concern for our health. The facts, however, suggest otherwise. Of far more relevant cause for concern is our willingness to jeopardize our health through damaging patterns of yo-yoing weight loss and re-gain; through stressful habits of "restrained eating," self-loathing, and stigmatization; through failures, whether we be fat or thin, to eat in a wholesome fashion and to exercise with full-bodied delight. If "health" were really the issue, we would be less punitive towards our own and each other's bodies, and more attuned to all our needs for pleasure and balance, rest and recreation. If health were really the issue, we would be less individualistic and capitalistic in our pursuit of bodily "perfection," and more committed to the corporate issues entailed in assuring that everyone in our society have access to adequate housing, nutrition, and medical care. If health were really the issue, far more of us could abandon the "five (or ten, or fifteen) pound fetish" and be satisfied to live within the upper limits of the weight range within which our bodies function comfortably. While we *cannot* all fit into the skinny end of the pear-shaped curve of weight distribution, we *can* all work to promote fuller human flourishing, body and soul.

In other words, we are not helpless. We simply need clearer prioritization of those matters which we can help, and those which we cannot. I am insisting, in concert with an increasing number of scientific authorities, that there are many people in our society who simply cannot help being fat. Even with moderate diet and appropriate exercise, their bodies—otherwise healthy—defend a set-point substantially higher than the "norm" (and their only way to achieve the norm would be to subsist on starvation rations henceforth and forevermore). According to George Blackburn, obesity specialist at Harvard Medical School: "At least half of obese people . . . who try to diet down to 'desirable' weights listed in the height-weight tables suffer medically, physically and psychologically as a result, and would be better off fat."[24]

But the intransigence of fatness need not translate into the intractability of food/diet addictions. All too often, people writing on "recovery" issues make a facile equation between the two, between "overweight" and "overeating"—and the result is an unfortunate confusion. The confusion seems to stem from the error of applying a uniform *medical* or *moral* model to issues of fatness and food addictions, rather than differentiating between the two. For example, there are those who readily acknowledge the physiological component to fatness, and who hasten to extend this analysis to eating compulsions. In more sophisticated scientific circles, such theorists search for "trait markers" indicative of a genetic underpinning to eating disorders, and they research the activity of neurotransmitters (hypothalamic beta-endorphin, 5-hydroxytryptamine serotonin) on the physiology of carbohydrate cravings.[25] In more everyday circles, they borrow the "disease model" of alcoholism, pathologizing the properties of certain foods (like sugar and refined flour) and modifying the slogan "one drink/one drunk" to something along the lines of "one bite/one binge."[26] In terms of this uniformly applied *medical* model, not only can many of us not help being fat; neither can we help our disordered eating patterns, apart from drug therapy and/or total abstinence from those foods which prove biochemically as well as psychologically addicting.

At the opposite extreme of the "uniformists" are those who apply a *moral* model both to fatness and to food/diet compulsions. These theorists start from the premise that "excessive appetites" are more rooted in life-style choices than in the chemical composition of those substances which seem so excessively, even addictively, appetizing.[27] They move from this rather hopeful, self-helpful perspective, however, to the rather judgmental conflation of food addiction with fatness, and vice versa. In their comprehensive presentation of (as they call it) *The Truth About Addiction and Recovery*, Stanton Peele and Archie Brodsky entitle their chapter on food-related addictions, "Obesity"—as if there were no thin food addicts; as if there were no fat people who were "normal," non-compulsive eaters. The first sentence of the chapter reads, "The addiction problem that affects the most Americans is eating and overweight."[28] Is this equation of issues intended to imply that compulsive eating is *not* a problem if it doesn't result in weight gain—or that so-called "overweight" *is* a problem even if a person is otherwise physically and psychologically healthy? The *moral* model, like the *medical* one, spreads unappetizingly thin when it is extended in this undifferentiated fashion.

What we need to do, I want to argue, is to distinguish more carefully the appropriate areas in which medical or moral models apply—to differentiate between those conditions which we cannot help, and those which we can. We *can* help the physiological factor of our set-point *to an extent*: by exercising, eating foods low in fats, and refraining from the temptation to engage sporadically in low-calorie dieting. We do not have complete control, however, over such other physiological givens as metabolism, build, number of fat cells in our bodies, and tendencies to convert calories into stored fat rather than into expended energy. In short, many "*medical*" factors pertaining to fatness cannot be helped—nor need they be helped, given new and non-prejudicial understandings about the relationship between physical size and physical well-being.[29]

On the other hand, attitudes toward fatness do fall within our control—although, granted, effecting a shift in attitudes is no simple matter when the entire weight of our culture presses (oppresses) us in the direction of fat-phobia and the worship of thinness as a mini-god. *Furthermore*, along with proponents of a moral model, I want to contend that attitudes and actions related to food and diet are amenable to control. I make this claim in part as a student of the literature on eating disorders (and there is good reason for calling them "disorders" and not "diseases," to which I shall return in a moment). I also make it as a person in recovery: I used to binge and purge regularly and excruciatingly, but do so no longer; I used to fear that one bite of refined carbohydrate meant I would "blow" the whole day, but now I find I can eat pleasurably indulgent amounts of sugar or white flour and then stop; I used to hop from one diet to another, with my weight yo-yoing within a twenty-pound range, whereas now I have stopped dieting and remained at a stable weight (within a three to five pound variance) for over six years; I used to hate my shape and size, but now, much of the time, I feel at peace with—and even celebrative of—the embodied self which I have been given. Finally, I make the claim that food-related behaviors can be "helped" as a Christian theologian: not one who wants to assess whether "fat Christians" are or are not "walking with the Lord," but rather, one who is convinced that our human powers to "help ourselves" are further empowered by a divine grace which lifts us out of fear and frantic behaviors into affirmation and fullness of life.

We are not helpless over food. I realize that this assertion contradicts a foundational premise of Overeaters Anonymous, that recovery group for compulsive overeaters founded on the model of Alcoholics Anonymous and adapting the "disease model of addiction" to food-related matters. I certainly do not want to dispute the spiritual dimension of OA which emphasizes the importance of help from a "Higher Power" in overcoming addictive habits, nor do I wish to discount the degree of personal support which OA groups provide for people who are struggling to return food to a proportionate place in their living. My only quarrel is with the quasi-medical model of food abuse, whether it be employed by OA or others, which declares that "certain foods or types of foods are addictive for some people . . . [such that] the addicted eater . . . is 'powerless' over these foods—typically refined sugar—and must therefore avoid eating them altogether."[30]

Counter to the quasi-medical model, numerous authorities assert that sugar is *not* an addictive substance, that "there is no physiological proof that eating sugar leads one compulsively to eat more and more sugar."[31] This assertion does not deny the fact that there are physiological *components* to carbohydrate cravings (indeed, there are physiological components to everything about us, given that as humans, we are embodied beings). Eating carbohydrates, particularly in the quick-fix form of sugar, increases the amount of the amino acid tryptophan in our bodies, which in turn raises levels of serotonin in our brains, serving to decrease irritability and to create feelings of calm. But one telling factor militates against moving from this linkage between carbohydrates and mood-altering serotonin to a merely biological explanation of compulsive eating. Not only does the brain signal when it needs

134

more serotonin, but also when it has had enough; those of us who binge, tend to override these physiological signals of satiation with behavioral desires to keep on eating, for whatever variety of learned (and consequently, unlearnable) reasons. Hence, as Peele and Brodsky conclude in their critique of the disease model of food addiction, rather than "banning sugar," we should more appropriately learn "to be aware of how much sugar [we] are eating and to recognize how sugar affects [us]."[32]

In addition to arguments discounting the physically addictive properties of particular foods, there are other compelling reasons for preferring a moral model to a disease-oriented understanding of aberrant eating. While some theorists suggest that the success of anti-depressant medications in treating people who binge and purge lends "support for a more biological explanation of bulimia within the eating disorders community," others argue that the connection between depression and bulimia is more correlational than causal.[33] Indeed, a number of the physiological features associated with anorexia or bulimia may just as readily be understood as results, rather than causes, of the behavioral aberrations (results, for example, of stressing the body through starvation, or through yo-yoing patterns of underindulgence and overindulgence, weight loss and weight gain). Biochemical factors alone certainly cannot account for the sudden upswing in the incidence of eating disorders during the last decades of the twentieth century. Rather, it seems clear that a number of factors related to issues of consumerism, control (particularly of women's bodies and psyches), and cultic devotion to the "god of thinness" have combined to generate the current "epidemic" of food and diet addictions. Hence, it makes more sense to understand these addictions as behavioral disorders and as "culture-bound syndromes" rather than as biomedical diseases.[34]

The final, and most serious problem with the medical model of disordered eating is that it encourages an evasion of responsibility, at both corporate and individual levels. Corporate evasion takes the form of a tendency to view addiction as the addict's problem alone, palming off any responsibility for effecting change onto the victim/patient and the hoped-for "silver bullet" of a medical cure. If it is only the "obese," or the "biochemically" bulimic or anorexic person who has a food addiction problem, then the rest of us who are not "overweight" or are not binging and purging on a daily basis can conveniently overlook our own calorie-counting and scale-watching obsessions, and our own contributions to the cultural deification of slenderness.

As with society at large, so with the individual: the medical model of food/diet addictions fosters an evasive and shoulder-shrugging response of, "I just can't help myself." Maybe I cannot help the extraordinary, evolutionarily adaptive efficiency of my body at using as few calories as possible to sustain basal functioning so that it can lay down the rest as fat to keep me warm and nourished through the next Ice Age, the next Potato Famine. Maybe I can't help a number of facts about my girth. Still, I *can* help my gluttony. Proponents of the moral model of addictions point to the evidence of numbers of people who simply "mature out" of destructive behaviors.[35] However entrenched my patterns of compulsive eating and dieting may be, there is significant reason to believe that I *learned* these patterns as ways of coping with the stresses of my life-situation, and that I can consequently *unlearn* them as I work to develop more sensuously responsible and responsibly sensuous patterns of appropriating the goods (and the "goodies") of the earth.

In short, I am not helpless; we are not helpless. We can help ourselves out of destructive attitudes toward food and diet, fatness and thinness. Before we turn to investigate the processes through which such self-help can occur, however, three caveats are in order. The first is that even though the disease model is flawed as an exclusive explanation for the causes of food addictions, a medical orientation does have its usefulness: it is important that we understand how the chemical properties of certain foods affect our bodies and our moods; and it is imperative that we provide and procure medical care for the serious physiological complications brought on by long-term food abuse. Second, the preference of a moral to a medical moral of addictive behaviors should not be taken as an excuse for *moralizing*. As Lloyd Steffen remarks in his review of Herbert Fingarette's work on alcohol abuse, "Locating problem drinking [or eating] in the moral universe neither legitimates simplistic judgmentalism nor authorizes a lack of compassion; rather, it asks that a sober look be taken at a self-destructive behavior so that the desires giving rise to it can be squarely and honestly addressed."[36] Third, as we work to avoid judgmentalism, we can be spurred by the recognition that neither maladaptive behaviors nor recovery from such behaviors can arise in a vacuum: self-destructiveness emerges in response to environmental stresses, and "self-help" requires significant help from others. The process of "maturing out" of problematic eating patterns ultimately becomes a process of spiritual maturation, and requires a balance of personal effort, communal support, and divinely empowering grace.

HOW CAN WE HELP?

Nearly six months ago, on the self-hating morning after a granola binge, I started writing this book. Now, as I approach the final section of the final chapter, it seems appropriate to pause and take stock of my situation once again. Over the past six months, intriguing things have been happening—the kind of personal transformations I would expect to discover in a fictional character before the close of a novel, but would be rather suspicious of in other contexts: they would seem forced to me, a little too "neat." But here they are: over the past six months, I have largely stopped feeling disgruntled with my body size and shape, stopped thinking I need to lose just "five more pounds," stopped thinking at every moment I really should be on a diet, stopped bingeing and hating myself thereafter . . . Instead of these formerly habitual and destructive activities, I have begun on an increasingly regular basis to look in the mirror and like what I see, to decide how I will feed myself on a given day based on how full or empty my body feels rather than on what weight the scale declares that I am, to replace thoughts of dieting with deep breaths of freedom, to eat the foods I really desire with pleasure and gratitude rather than guilt (and to stop eating them when I feel full rather than stuffing myself beyond satiation). Perhaps most importantly of all, I have stopped reacting to other people as well as to myself with instinctive and judgmental weightism, and I have begun seeing the bodies of all those I meet as right and beautiful after their own distinctive fashions.

Tales of transformations. In light of this ongoing personal conversion, I am moved to suggest—only partially tongue in cheek—that perhaps every compulsive eater and dieter seeking recovery should attempt to write a book about the process. Perhaps all of us who have been size-obsessed should form a coalition to pressure the publishing industry into imposing a moratorium on diet books, printing instead the testimonials of those of us who are finding our way out of eating and diet obsessions. I suspect that as a result of such a shift in publishing focus, just as many pounds would ultimately be shed (if that is even a by-product worth mentioning), more natural and stable set-points would be reached, more people would be empowered to love themselves, body and soul, and our society would become in general healthier place in which to live.

I will not, of course, hold my breath—nor will I attempt a hunger strike until such time as that change in priorities occurs. There is simply too much good food to enjoy, and too many good people in whose company to enjoy it. Still, I will suggest here in closing a few important interim measures which we can take, a few fruits of the Spirit which we can savor on the road to recovery from eating compulsions, this side of the fruit trees of Eden and this side of the banquet of the Lamb. Those fruits have to do with the cultivation of new habits and new hopes; the ripening of trust; and the reaping and repeating of daily graces through which we all may be more fittingly fed.

New Habits and New Hopes

Gluttony is a bad habit. There is no simpler way of putting the issue. But, for the sake of balance, I must remind us all of the fact that in the Christian tradition, gluttony has as much to do with patterns of excessive abstinence as it does with patterns of excessive indulgence. For spiritual directors like Evagrius, Cassian, and Gregory, any habit of consumption or non-consumption that violates the values of community spirit, self-control, and grateful care for the creation qualifies as gluttonous. For a scholastic theologian like Thomas Aquinas, any failure to order our pleasures and our renunciations with concern for our bodily health, attention to our neighbors, and devotion to the goodness of God qualifies as sinfully "intemperate." For all these thinkers, the excesses of gluttony figure among the "cardinal" or "deadly" sins because they do not limit themselves to passing moments of indulgence. Rather, they expand, becoming dispositions of character, chronic ways of misappropriating the goods of the earth. In short, they become long-lasting and destructive *habits*.[37]

As habits, patterns of compulsive eating and compulsive dieting are deeply entrenched in our ways of acting and thinking and being in the world. But as habits, they are also amenable to change; we are not finally helpless under their sway. Indeed, it is a fundamental premise of Christian moral theology that *conversion* is a real, even a promising, possibility—and "maturing out" of a destructive habit is very much like the conversion process of becoming a "new creature." As such, it involves both a modification of behaviors and a re-visioning of deeply held hopes and beliefs.

We can change. Over the course of a lifetime, we do, in fact, acquire new skills and new self-images, new relationships and new ways of understanding the world. Emerging out of a compulsive relationship to food entails making intentional efforts in all these areas, as well as being open to receiving the grace that supplements our best efforts when they seem doomed to fail. There are still moments—though they come less frequently than they did even a mere six months ago—when I catch myself in the dread of Ellen West, the dread of eating and of not-eating alike: when I am hurting and I wish I could turn to food, but I know it simply would not offer sufficient or lasting comfort any more. And I grow angry at the hurting, angry at the emptiness, wishing I could swallow down the pain in old, familiar ways. But sometimes, in those very moments, a curiously defiant peacefulness descends—and the moment passes, and I find I have coped beyond my known abilities at coping, and I feel renewed.

So, grace and effort, struggle and surprise must both attend any conversion process. A major part of the struggle entails the effort to learn new coping skills. Anyone who acquires an eating or dieting compulsion does so for a reason. The behavior serves a purpose: it relieves monotony, dulls anxiety, deflects attention from an unmanageable problem to a more familiar one; it focuses enormous amounts of mental and emotional energy; it supplies an identity and a culturally-approved set of almost-reachable dreams. To change the habit first requires recognizing the important functions it has served, even being *grateful* for the ways in which it has proved a boon in difficult life-situations. ("In all things, give thanks. . . . ") Then, it involves the spiritually demanding task of discovering new and healthier ways to fill these needed functions. The new ways will not be the same for everyone, just as the prior patterns of destructive coping were not the same. (I used to binge on bowlfuls of white flour, salt, and Wesson Oil, all mixed together. I have yet to hear of anyone else who ever binged in quite this fashion—nor do I expect anyone else's recovery to follow a path identical to mine.) Recall Margaret Miles's definition of spiritual practices (cited in the first chapter) as "exercises, carefully chosen and individually tailored to address a particular person's compulsive behavior, addictions, or destructive thought patterns."[38]

Individually tailored behavioral changes are important: throwing food away rather than enacting the crazy compulsion to eat "the whole thing," as if somehow any excess would be less "wasted" in an already sated stomach than in a garbage can; going for a walk instead of eating, when the desire for food is rooted in anxiety or boredom rather than in physical hunger; giving the bathroom scales to a friend who is not size-obsessed and therefore will not turn them into an altar before which to perform daily sacrifices of serenity and self-esteem.[39] But behavioral changes must be accompanied by attitudinal changes, by shifts in self-imaging and in ways of making sense of the world: because the bad habit of gluttony—whether it takes shape in compulsive indulgence or in compulsive abstinence—roots just as much in distortions of thought as in distortions of activity.

For example, here is a list of four habitual patterns of thinking that haunt the minds of those of us with problematic attitudes toward food and diet:

1. If I'm not perfect, I'm a terrible person. (If I eat a hundred "extra" calories, a single bite of a "forbidden" food, I've blown

the whole day and I'm a failure; I've failed so many times that I even wonder if life is worth the effort of living.)

2. If I don't look right, people won't like me. (I weigh two pounds more this morning than I did yesterday and everyone is going to notice that my skirt is too tight around the waist. People will stare at me and think how fat and ugly and disgusting I am.)

3. If people really knew me, they wouldn't approve of me. (I must lie to the checker at the grocery store about why I'm buying so much food. I must hide my binges [or my abstinence] from my housemates, my family. I must not eat "too much" in public. I must always appear to be "normal" and in control.)

4. If I didn't have food to turn to, I wouldn't be able to handle the other problems of my life. (I wouldn't know what to do with my open time, my loneliness, my anger, my pain. At least food gives me some comfort; at least a regimented diet gives me some sense of purpose and some structure.)

In these four examples of cognitive distortions which accompany eating disorders, we can see a number of even deeper issues—spiritual issues—at work: absolutist expectations; idolatrous approval-seeking; evasion of intimacy; and dread of emptiness.

Absolutist expectations. Food and diet addictions thrive on all-or-nothing thinking: either I'm adhering perfectly to my regimen, or I'm a failure; either I'm in absolute control, or I'm in frantic abandon; either I'm busy every moment, or I'm wasting time (even eating, ironically, counts as "busyness"); either I weigh whatever magic number of pounds (my eschatological "goal weight"), or I'm grotesque; either other people conform to the societal norm of slenderness, or they're sloppy, piggish, and lazy. There is little in this mindset that allows for ambiguity, nuance, or forgiveness. This is *hubris* at work—that old snake in the grass of seductively hissing *pride*.

To counter pride requires the work of spiritual discipline, the effort to learn patience, humility, and paradox. At one and the same time, I am both sinner and saint, both a disordered eater and a person on the road to recovery. I falter, and I regain my footing, over and over again—and the lessons from the faltering can be as precious as the moments of easy traveling. I do not always have to be taking the high road, looking out in watchful judgment over myself or others; sometimes, I can simply pause by the wayside and let matters *be*, accepting and even rejoicing in the given. I can temper my absolute expectations for myself with a more modest and dynamic hopefulness—the desire for progress rather than for perfection. I can work and pray, alone and in community, to find a more ultimately sustaining hope, a better eschatological goal than that of losing "just five more pounds."

Idolatrous approval-seeking. It is, of course, idolatry to import a pseudo-ultimate significance onto the number on the scale, to let my weight on a given day determine my moody manner of working and of relating to others. It is idolatry to invest certain foods with magical properties (whether angelic—like grapefruit, or demonic—like refined white sugar), or to invest certain rituals regarding food (whether purging with emetics or counting calories) with proto-salvific powers.[40] It is idolatry to be so "conformed to this age" that the cultural standards of beauty and acceptability come to dominate my every waking thought.

Numbers are not magic; foods are not magic; dieting rituals are not a route to ultimate salvation (nor even to physical health and well-being). We can help ourselves in overcoming food and diet addictions only when we learn to shift our focus away from *appearance* as a criterion of merit, and develop the habit of delving deeper into ourselves and others to find a more genuine and renewing, "transformative" Beauty.

Evasion of intimacy. When I am frightened that I do not and will never "fit" the cultural standard of acceptability, I become frightened that I am unacceptable in other ways as well. As a result, I begin hiding. I am fearful of letting my body be seen, even by a beloved. I am fearful of letting myself be known as I truly am—so I go to devious and destructive extremes to avoid being "found out." I starve myself in public and snitch food on the sly, because I do not want my real appetites to be apparent. I attempt to conceal my neediness, my hurts, my fears, my angers. Either I am so busy trying to please other people that I cannot be fully available to myself, or I am so busy trying to attend to the demands of my addiction that I cannot be fully available to other people. I lie to myself about the extent of my problem. I lie to others. I pull away from relationships, forgetting the fundamental dictum of my creation: "It is not good that the human creature should be alone."

If a food addiction festers in solitary hiding, its cure breathes in the open air of "coming out"—coming out of the pantry, out of the cupboard, out of the closet; coming out of the habit of hiding candy bars in a dresser drawer, or cleaning the bathroom meticulously so that no one will notice the signs of a purge, or driving to the grocery store to buy another carton of ice cream and then eating half of it, too, so that the remainder will look just like the carton of half-eaten ice cream that was in the freezer the night before . . . And coming out means not only owning up to the behaviors, but also to the hurtful mindsets that fuel and reinforce them: "I'm afraid you won't love me if I'm fat"; "I have to have *something* in my life that I can *control*"; "Sometimes I feel so lonely, I just don't know what else to do." To make a confession (before self, before some trusted other, before God) of the fullest extent of the pain is to begin the process of healing. Becoming honest means becoming *responsible*: not simply embracing appropriate accountability, but also seeking appropriate responsiveness—from self and others—to our most urgent hungers, which actually have little to do with food.

Dread of emptiness. Nowhere does the need for formulating new habits and new hopes to deal with a food addiction become more powerful or demanding than here—for it is the habitual hopelessness of dread that lurks, both literally and metaphorically, at the very core of disordered eating. In fact, this particular cognitive and spiritual distortion is so poignantly central to the dynamics of addiction that it requires a section of discussion unto itself.

Temperance, Temporality, and Trust

I do not like to feel empty. To feel empty is to feel abandoned, left alone at a time when I am yearning for the embrace of arms and of understanding. To feel empty is to feel lost, uprooted, adrift in airy nothingness, unsure of where to turn or what to do. To feel empty is to feel as if I have cried for so many days on end that there are not even any tears remaining, but all that is left inside me is a parched and red-raw cavern that aches and burns.

To feel empty is to wonder if there is any sense at all to this whole cosmic show which runs to tragedy over and over again, or any meaning to my own life which runs from depression to elation and back again at the slightest provocation, and sometimes with no apparent provocation at all. To feel empty is dread-full. I do not like it at all.

One way to deal with emptiness is to try to fill it—force feed it: metaphorically and literally. Fill it up with projects, with possessions, with relationships, with restless activity. Stuff it full with food. What do I do with empty time—time alone in the house, surrounded by jumbled stacks of four-by-six cards, waiting for an outline to emerge out of the void, staring at the blank and blipping computer screen (I think I know why they call that flashing neon rectangle a "cursor"!)? Eat granola! Numb the emptiness psychologically with the soothing ritual activity of moving spoon (or rather, fingers) from bowl to mouth, with rhythmic regularity. Numb the emptiness physiologically with the ingestion of sufficient sugar to release mood-altering serotonin in my brain. Muffle the rawness. Coat it with a thick pink layer of carbohydrate comfort.

Or what do I do when I am feeling dissatisfied with myself and my life, feeling at loose ends and out of control? What one activity perennially promises newness of life—the solution of all problems, the perfecting of all imperfections, the release from all loneliness through the final (eschatological) achievement of irresistible desirability? A new diet! *This* time things will be different. *This* time I will eat nothing but raw vegetables between meals; *this* time I will have "only a shake for breakfast and lunch, and then eat a sensible dinner." (The litanies are as familiar as the Psalms, are they not? or alas, perhaps far more familiar!) Forget the fact that my anxiety, my sense of lostness, has only the flimsiest of connections with my scale weight; forget the fact that I can feel just as lonely and depressed at 120 pounds as I can at 150. It is easier to look at the surface numbers than at the deeper chasm. It is easier to find something, anything at all, that I can pretend to *do*.

Only, the "doing" does not work (for all the physiological reasons that diets do not lastingly work, rehearsed in the first half of this chapter), and the "doing" does not touch the real problem.

The real problem is emptiness and dread of emptiness, and no amount of stuffing food or structuring a diet will ultimately take care of it. The only thing that will take care of it is *trust*, whose tender ripening makes possible an emergence out of the brokenness of addiction towards the wholeness of health.

Three forms of trust foster this emergence: trust in the rhythms of time, trust in the wisdom of our bodies, and trust in the fruitfulness of emptiness itself.

"To everything there is a season." In the first chapter above, we looked at the practical discipline taught by the Christian calendar in its rhythmic alternations of feast days and fast days, with "daily bread" days in between. The liturgical calendar gives formal recognition to the fact, also noted by Brian Grant in his analysis of gluttony, that:

> It is part of the natural rhythm of life to alternate between occasional magnificent excesses of self-indulgence, which remind us that this really is a rich and good world, and longer, ordinary periods.[41]

Or, conversely, it is also part of the natural rhythm of life to include periods of aridity and emptiness and unfulfilled yearning. The eating disordered person is woefully out of touch with all these rhythms.

Such "arrhythmia" can take quite concrete forms. Addiction researchers Scott Mizes and Robert Klesges note that one of the cognitive distortions central to anorexia nervosa and bulimia is an "inability to see alternating hunger and satiety as normal."[42]

In other words, when I as a bulimic or a compulsive eater and dieter feel hungry, I experience a panicky fear that the discomfort will last forever, and so I seek urgently, frantically to dispel it.[43] Immediate gratification becomes critical: I do not even have time to take off my coat when I walk in the door of my house, to transfer food from its carton to a serving dish, to sit down at my dining room table. Or, on the other hand, when I as an eating disordered person feel full, even after a normal-sized meal, I fear that I have stuffed myself irredeemably—that my stomach will always feel this heavy and rounded, that my clothes will always feel this tight. And so, I must either purge immediately in order to do away with the unpleasant feeling of satiety, or I must instantly begin recalculating my diet—how little I will eat for the next meal or the next day in order to "compensate." I feel the constant need to be doing something, correcting something; I cannot simply trust to the passage of time and of living to carry me naturally from fullness to hunger and from hunger to fullness again.

In his book on *The Deadly Diet: Recovering from Anorexia and Bulimia*, Terence Sandbek aptly observes: "One of the most difficult things for the Deadly Dieter to control is time."[44] Not just in its rhythms of literal, physical hunger and satiation, but also in its rhythms of metaphorical emptiness and plenitude, time can be terrifying to the compulsion-prone person. I know. Eating (or bingeing and purging, or calculating and recalculating a diet) at least passes the time: the time between ideas and the emergence of outlines, the time between letters or phone calls from loved ones, the time between activities and accomplishments, the time between full-fillments of one sort or another. There is a fund of deep insight in the fact that the word *temperance* and the word *temporality* share an etymological root (*tempus*): for temperance—whether it has to do with the embrace of indulgence or of abstinence in due measure—stems from the patient ability to allow time to impart its own seasons and seasonings to my living. Constant eating, or constant dieting, is intemperate (and "ill-tempered"), precisely because it has forgotten how to *wait* for the fullness of time.

A kindred etymological insight is couched in the words *attend* (archaically, "to wait for") and *attention*: both involve a figurative stretching toward (*ad* plus *tendere*), a well-tempered heeding. Just as patient waiting, attuned to the pacing and the passing of time, forms a key ingredient of trust, so too does perceptive attention and attunement to the body's needs and teachings. Where the first chapter above named feasting and fasting as importantly alternating disciplines which help me relate to food with more sensuous responsibility, it also named "fine-tuning" as the practice of becoming more aware of my bodily wisdom. In a bold rejection of gnosticism (and all its lip-curling simplicity), Christian theology persistently refuses to locate evil within the physical body. Rather, as God's creation (and as the locus for ongoing incarnation), the body itself is good. Evil enters the world with perversion of the *will*, with the destructive desire to consume forbidden fruits of power and pleasure which I do not need, which I cannot rightfully enjoy, and which I am not wise enough to handle.

There are many areas in which it would scarcely occur to me *not* to trust my body. The most obviously relevant example is thirst. I know when my mouth is dry and I need a glass of water. I also know when I have drunk enough to quench my physical craving without continuing to gulp and guzzle until my stomach is painfully distended. Why do I not have the same, sure knowledge of my appetite for food?

The answer lies in perversion of the will. Some of this perversion is born of greed, of gluttony, of wanting to take more into myself than I need for sustenance, or even for simple pleasure. But often, particularly in the eating disordered person, beneath the gluttony lies a seeming paradox: the fact that the perverse urge to overconsume is born not so much of excessive self-indulgence as of obsessive self-restraint. The more willfully I try to control my hungers, the more I experience their backlash. Psychological research on "restrained" versus "unrestrained" eaters has verified this phenomenon: it is the restrained eater, the one who is always counting calories and refusing dessert (in public) who is the most inclined to binge (in private) in response to emotional cues rather than physical hungers; the unrestrained eater, who eats what she wants when she wants it, is also able to forego eating when her body is not physically hungry.[45] The perversity of constant restraint manifests a destructively spiraling *scrupulosity*: the more meticulously I calculate every mouthful of food, the more enmeshed I become in the machinations of my self-will. This is "caloric Pelagianism" at work—the dubious and ultimately doomed attempt to "save myself" through extraordinary works of dietary righteousness.[46] I cannot heal an obsession with food by replacing it with a counterobsession with dieting. The only way I can be healed is to stop my obsessive doing, and start trusting instead.

Trusting, for example, that my body not only knows *when* it is hungry, but *what* it is hungry for. It takes time to relearn these signals, after a lifetime of ignoring them in favor of some artificially imposed regimen or some rebounding rhythm of under- and overindulgence. A number of recent writers on the process of recovery from compulsive eating offer tips and techniques for developing an approach to "demand feeding for adults" which re-attunes itself to the body's own needs and requirements. Among the most helpful of these authors are Jane Hirschmann and Carol Munter (coiners of the phrase, "demand feeding"), Marion Bilich, Susan Kano, Susie Orbach, and Geneen Roth.[47] The necessary circularity of this technique is that it both takes and teaches trust: it takes trust to stop dieting and start eating what I want when I want it; it takes trust to *stop* eating when I first reach fullness, calming my irrational fears that food, especially the particular food that I am eating at the moment, will never be available to me again; yet, it also teaches trust to reassure myself, each time I eat on body-felt demand, that a wisdom deeper than my willful ego knows, in a divinely-created way, what is best for me. As Hirschmann and Munter put it:

> Each time you feed yourself when your stomach is hungry, you are accomplishing two important tasks—nourishing yourself physiologically and nurturing yourself emotionally. You are repeating an event which, from infancy on, has symbolized trust. Indeed, feeding yourself appropriately satisfies two most basic human needs, those of physical and emotional sustenance.[48]

I would, of course, add that this process satisfies a deep need for *spiritual* sustenance as well. As I learn to feed myself fittingly, I also learn to refrain from the temptation to feed myself *un*-fittingly. In so doing, I practice an attunement that counters my eager seeking after anaesthesia. I learn to open myself to my experiences rather than stuff them down with mouthfuls of pain-numbing food. In short, I begin to discover how to let myself be *empty*.

And the discovery of emptiness is a fruit of the Spirit, indeed—a precious, if poignant, gift. If I can stop force-feeding myself long enough to feel the full range of my hungers, both physical and spiritual, I can discover in those hungers a passionate longing—a longing which reminds me how I am not intended to find complete satisfaction in the brokenness and limitations of life this side of the garden of Eden. This side of the garden of Eden and this side of the consummate banquet of the Lamb, my heart is meant to be yearning and restless. Recall the words of Augustine, cited in the first chapter above, *On the Usefulness of Fasting*:

> When people are hungry, they stretch out toward something; while they are stretching, they are enlarged; while they are enlarged, they become capacious, and when they have become capacious enough, they will be filled in due time.[49]

No one carries forward this Augustinian wisdom better than Gerald May in his book on the healing of human hungers, *Addiction and Grace*. "Our incompleteness," May writes, "is the empty side of our longing for God and for love. It is what draws us to God and one another."[50] If we never felt empty, we would never need God or other people. If we never felt empty, we would never experience within ourselves the spaciousness into which grace can pour. If there were no empty room in our heart, in our innermost parts, there would be no room for sacred nativity.

So we must learn to trust not only to the rhythms of time and the wisdom of our own bodies, but also to the paradoxical fruitfulness of emptiness itself. This is probably the most difficult lesson of all. It requires patience, and watchfulness, and courage. It requires letting go and letting be. It requires a cessation of all the frantic, evasive tactics that keep me from coming face to face with myself, face to face with all the fierceness and fragility of my love-hungry, God-hungry heart. Listen to the words of one who knows both the fearfulness and the daring:

> What do [we] do with [our] hungers? The voice at the center of the vortex that calls [us], beckons [us] to follow its spiraling down, down to the starkness, the rawness? [We] may drink or take drugs, or [we] eat. . . . It's all the same. We all run. We are all afraid of our own hungers.
>
> Except the ones who aren't. The madmen, the artists, the saints. They walk right into the starkness. . . . They become, they actually become, the space between one breath and another. The madmen stay mad because they are caught in the eye of the center, whirling. . . . The artists, the saints, get to the other side. No longer afraid of their own hungers, they seem to live at the center of a sparkle that brightens and dims according to a natural rhythm. But

even the madmen are ahead of us: at least they leap. We would rather turn to food or drugs or drink that dulls the call, never reaching the loamy hungers inside.[51]

The loamy hungers frighten us. And yet, the loamy hungers are the soil in which seeds of grace can be planted to grow into the artist and the saint that each one of us is beckoned to be. Paradoxically and importantly, we must work at letting ourselves spiral down into the starkness and emptiness, in order that our work may be supplanted by a peace that surpasses our own powers, and in order that our deepest hungers may be divinely fed.

Daily Graces

So, fearfulness and daring, effort and relaxation, emptiness and fullness, struggle and surprise . . . In the end, all our endeavours to help ourselves in recovery from food addictions come down to a final word—and the word is *grace*: Grace as gift, and grace as thanksgiving. We *receive* grace from the hand of God and by the hands of one other in the support which sustains us in our struggles to be freed of gluttony, to learn to appropriate the goods of the earth in a manner which is both fit and fulfilling. And we *say* grace when we sit down to our tables, alone or in company, as a means of expressing thanks for the struggles and the blessings of our lives.

For the eating disordered person, the reaping and repeating of "daily graces" bears particular importance for the ongoing process of recovery. *Reaping* grace empowers the long journey out of addiction and into health—the trial and error, the gradual growth in consciousness and in confidence, the forgiveness that embraces failure and enables starting over again. How many times have I begun a new pattern of eating, vowing to myself that, "*This* time, things will be different," only to find that after a few fervid days or weeks, I slip back into old, familiar habits? How many times have I felt the utter discouragement that tells me I might as well give up, because I can never change? How many times has a single set-back tempted me to abandon hope that my life can ever be made new? How many times will I *keep* needing to be healed

151

of these bad habits of absolutist thinking, letting go of my harsh demands and my bitter disappointments with myself, letting the grace of forgiveness invigorate me daily, hourly, to start afresh and refreshed?

And *repeating* daily graces is a ritual with extraordinary aptness as a spiritual discipline for an eating disordered person on the journey of recovery. Every meal, every mouthful becomes a blessed opportunity to practice bodily and spiritual attunement. Pausing to "say grace" enables pausing to feel the precise hungers in my being—whether they be for food or for some other satisfaction altogether: rest, recreation, companionship, touch. Pausing to "say grace" enables pausing to anticipate and appreciate the celebrative savor of food. The liturgical act of formulating a "grace"—whether it be spoken aloud or received in silence—provides an opportunity for training my imagination in new ways of visualizing myself and new ways of envisioning the world. To pray is to seek words and silences that can help me to retrain my hungers, my habits, and my hopes.

And so, it is fitting to end by "saying grace." I offer here two graces, one by Robert Farrar Capon, and one of my own. In preparing his, Capon laments the dietary fetishes that have plagued us in our cultural subservience to the "god of thinness." In their place, he offers "a little prayer for the return of sanity to our tables":

> O Lord, refresh our sensibilities. Give us this day our daily taste. . . . Take away our fear of fat, and make us glad of the oil which ran upon Aaron's beard. Give us pasta with a hundred fillings, and rice in a thousand variations. Above all, give us the grace to live as true men [and women]—to fast till we come to a refreshed sense of what we have and then to dine gratefully on all that comes to hand. . . . Deliver us from the fear of calories . . . and set us free once more in our own land, where we shall serve thee as thou hast blessed us—with the dew of heaven, the fatness of the earth, and plenty of corn and wine. Amen.[1]

Let all God's people respond, resoundingly, "Amen!"

Before saying grace for myself—at the ending of this book, and at the beginning of the rest of my love-hate struggle with food—I pause to note that each person at each moment has his or her own joys and tasks and discouragements and thanksgivings. Ready-to-say blessings may be about as hazardous to our well-being as ready-to-wear clothing has been. Despite my appreciation for the formal liturgies of the church, I doubt that there is finally any such thing as a "one size fits all" prayer. Rather, each of us must tailor our own—even as each of us must tailor our own living, in harmony with the variform bodies which we have been given, and in response to the distinctive lives of artistry and sainthood to which we are continually being called.

That said, here is a "daily grace," a little prayer for the retraining of hopes and the returning of food to its proper perspective:

> Gracious God of Word and of Table, to You be thanks and praise!
> For the garden of the earth, filled with all manner of things that are pleasing to the eye and delightful to the tongue:
> For fruits in their seasons—apples and melons; figs, grapes, and pomegranates; plums and oranges and peaches dripping with nectar;
> For seasonings and spices—almond and vanilla; cinnamon, clove, and nutmeg; rosemary and marjoram; bay leaf and oregano and thyme;
> For fellow creatures with whom to share the fruitfulness of the garden and the responsibility for tending it with care;
> For my own body, born of the earth by Your hands and animated by Your breath; for attentiveness to its incarnate rhythms and attunement to its good senses and good sense;
> For the serenity to hush my anxiety over appearances, my fretfulness about "conforming" to the standards of this age;
> For the insight to be "transformed" into appreciation of a more richly variegated beauty;
> For the patience to forgive myself, the strength to ask for help, and the stamina to take up my life-tasks over and over again;
> For the capacity to savor food with pleasure and gratitude, and to stop when I have eaten to my fill;
> For the wisdom to discern in my appetites a deeper hunger which opens me to others and to grace;
> For the courage and vigor to work more heartily that all may be fittingly fed;

THE GOD OF THINNESS

For the restless longing to join with all of creation in the final
banquet of the Lamb, feasting to fullness on Your presence,
singing over and over again:

Glory to the Source of all blessedness and all bounty!

Glory to the Sapience which teaches true tasting!

Glory to the Spirit which breathes into empty spaces and brings
renewal of life!

De profundis, gloria! In excelsis, gloria! Deo gloria! Deo gratias!
Amen.

NOTES

Apéritif: Frozen Yoga

1. Roger Campbell, *Thin, Trim, and Triumphant: How to Get God's Help in Losing Unwanted Pounds* (Wheaton, IL: Victor Books, 1989), especially pp. 63–67.

2. As the most outstanding collection of such writings, see Lisa Shoenfielder and Barb Wieser, eds., *Shadow on a Tightrope: Writings by Women on Fat Oppression* (San Francisco: Spinsters/Aunt Lute Book Company, 1983).

3. Geneen Roth, *Feeding the Hungry Heart: The Experience of Compulsive Eating* (New York: New American Library, 1982), p. 72.

4. Pope's *Homer*. Epigraph from M. F. K. Fisher, *Here Let Us Feast: A Book of Banquets* (San Francisco: North Point Press, 1986), p. xv.

First Course: Food for Thought

1. For kindred interpretations of the "gnostic" element in contemporary eating behaviors, see W. Stephen Sabom, "The Gnostic World of Anorexia Nervosa," *Journal of Psychology and Theology*, vol. 13, no. 4 (Winter 1985), pp. 243–254; and Robert Farrar Capon, *Health, Money, and Love, and Why We Don't Enjoy Them* (Grand Rapids, MI: Eerdmans, 1990), p. 155:

> The religions of health, money, and love—and of sex, romance, marriage, work, dieting, eating, jogging, or working out—all function as *mystery cults*. They are presented to us as possessing a secret *gnosis*, a private knowledge to be carefully guarded by the elect and to be extended to the general run of humanity only after the most exacting initiation rites. . . .

2. Albert Stunkard, "The Obese: Background and Programs," *Nutrition Policies in the 70s*, cited by Roberta Pollack Seid in *Never Too Thin:*

Why Women Are at War with Their Bodies (New York: Prentice Hall, 1989), p. 166.

3. See Seid, pp. 225–226, and Hillel Schwartz, *Never Satisfied: A Cultural History of Diets, Fantasies, and Fat* (New York: The Free Press, A Division of Macmillan, 1986), pp. 248–250.

4. See Barry Glassner, *Bodies: Why We Look the Way We Do (and How We Feel About It)* (New York: G. P. Putnam's Sons, 1988), p. 47.

5. See Glassner, p. 187.

6. Rita Freedman, *Bodylove: Learning to Like Our Looks–and Ourselves* (New York: Harper and Row, 1988), p. 82.

7. See Freedman, p. 82; Seid, p. 257; "Feeling Fat in a Thin Society," *Glamour* (February 1984), pp. 198–201.

8. The "relentless pursuit of thinness" is the classic definition given for anorexia nervosa by specialist Hilde Bruch. See, for example, her widely read and definitive work *The Golden Cage: The Enigma of Anorexia Nervosa* (New York: Vintage Books, 1979), p. ix. For further statistics, see excerpts from Naomi Wolf, *The Beauty Myth* (London: Chatto and Windus, 1990), printed in *The Sunday Times* [London] (September 9, 1990), Section 8, pp. 1–2; also see Seid, p. 21.

9. See Seid, p. 21; Wolf, p. 1; also Marlene Boskind-White, "Bulim-arexia: A Sociocultural Perspective," in *Theory and Treatment of Anorexia Nervosa and Bulimia: Biomedical, Sociocultural, and Psychological Perspectives*, ed. Steven Wiley Emmett (New York: Brunner/Mazel, 1985), p. 113.

10. Arnold Andersen, "Males with Eating Disorders," in *Eating Disorders*, ed. by Felix E. F. Larocca (San Francisco: Jossey-Bass, Inc., 1986), p. 40.

11. Report findings cited by Kay Sheppard in *Food Addiction: The Body Knows* (Deerfield Beach, FL: Health Communications, Inc., 1989), p. 59.

12. Mike Wallace, cited by Judith Moore, in "Bulimia: Catharsis or Curse?" *Witness*, vol. 66, No. 1 (January 1983), p. 14.

13. "The Big Business of Weight Loss," *NAAFA* [National Association to Advance Fat Acceptance] *Newsletter*, vol. xx, no. 1 (September 1990), p. 4.

14. Glassner, pp. 187 and 13.

15. Seid, p. 4.

16. Freeman, p. 82; Mary Catherine and Robert Tyson, quoted by Seid, p. 171; Seid, p. 276; Schwartz, p. 246, my emphasis.

17. Ludwig Binswanger, "The Case of Ellen West," cited by Craig Johnson and Mary Connors in *The Etiology and Treatment of Bulimia Nervosa: A Biopsychological Perspective* (New York: Basic Books, 1987), p. 4. Kim Chernin devotes an entire chapter to "The Mysterious Case of Ellen

West" in her groundbreaking book *The Obsession: Reflections on the Tyranny of Slenderness* (New York: Harper and Row, 1981).

18. M. F. K. Fisher, *The Art of Eating* (New York: Random House, Vintage Books Edition, 1976), p. 9.

19. Fisher, p. 42.

20. Roy Porter, Preface to Piero Camporesi, *Bread of Dreams: Food and Fantasy in Early Modern Europe*, trans. David Gentilcore (Chicago: University of Chicago Press, 1989), p. 10.

21. A "heuristic" or metaphorical theology is one which plays out the implications of particular metaphors or images for constructing (or reconstructing) an understanding of the ways in which God and the world interrelate. For a fuller explanation of this kind of theology, see Sallie McFague, *Models of God* (Philadelphia: Fortress Press, 1987), especially pp. xi–xii and pp. 35–37. McFague explores the metaphors of God as Mother, Lover, and Friend and of the world as God's body. In kindred but more abbreviated fashion, I am exploring the orienting and reconstructive images of God as Feeder and the world as God-given food.

22. For such images of a feeding "Mother Jesus," see Carolyn Bynum, *Holy Feast and Holy Fast* (Berkeley: University of California Press, 1987), especially plates 26 ff.

23. Phyllis Trible, *God and the Rhetoric of Sexuality* (Philadelphia: Fortress Press, 1978), pp. 87–88.

24. Robert Farrar Capon, *The Supper of the Lamb* (Garden City, NY: Doubleday and Co., 1969), pp. 86 and 114–115, and *Food for Thought* (New York: Harcourt, Brace, Jovanovich, 1978), pp. 28–29.

25. Matthew Fox, *Original Blessing* (Santa Fe, NM: Bear and Co., 1983), p. 62. Fox cites from von Rad, *Wisdom in Israel*, on p. 203.

26. Frank Bottomley, *Attitudes to the Body in Western Christendom* (London: Lepus Books, 1979), pp. 170–171.

27. Susie Orbach, *Hunger Strike: The Anorectic's Struggle as a Metaphor for Our Age* (New York: Avon Books, 1986).

28. For a thorough and fascinating (and thoroughly fascinating) exposition of these arguments, see especially Dorothy Dinnerstein, *The Mermaid and the Minotaur* (New York: Harper and Row, 1976).

29. Dalma Heyn, "Body Hate," *Ms.* (July/August 1989), p. 36.

30. See any one of a number of important books by Chernin, including *The Obsession*, cited above; *The Hungry Self* (New York: Times Books, Random House, 1985); and *Reinventing Eve: Modern Woman in Search of Herself* (New York: Harper and Row, 1987). Orbach's equally important titles include *Fat Is a Feminist Issue* (New York: Berkley Books, 1978); *Fat Is a Feminist Issue II* (New York: Berkley Books, 1982); and *Hunger Strike*, cited above.

31. Carl and LaVonne Braaten, *The Living Temple: A Practical Theology of the Body and the Foods of the Earth* (New York: Harper and Row, 1976), p. xiii.

32. Orbach, *Fat Is a Feminist Issue*, pp. 145-146.

33. Augustine, *De utilitate jejunii* 1, cited by Margaret Miles in *Practicing Christianity: Critical Perspectives for an Embodied Spirituality* (New York: Crossroad, 1990), p. 96.

34. Gerald May discusses this dynamic brilliantly in his analysis of *Addiction and Grace* (New York: Harper and Row, 1988).

35. Fisher, *The Art of Eating*, p. 321.

36. Miles, p. 9.

37. Miles, p. 94. See also Bottomley, p. 159

38. Gregary Palamas, *Homilies*, cited by Miles, p. 147.

39. For a helpful summary of Weber's categories, see Don Browning, *The Moral Context of Pastoral Care* (Philadelphia: Westminster, 1976), pp. 43-44.

40. For the definitive texts on medieval "anorexia," see Bynum, *Holy Feast and Holy Fast*, and Rudolph Bell, *Holy Anorexia* (Chicago: University of Chicago Press, 1985). The latter work has a particularly helpful epilogue by William Davis, a clinical psychologist who specializes in the psychotherapy of anorexia, who draws some enlightening comparisons and contrasts between medieval "holy anorexics" and the modern-day sufferers of eating disorders.

41. Miles, pp. 103-104, and explanatory note, p. 194.

42. Miles, p. 94.

43. Fox, *Original Blessing*, pp. 206-207.

44. Fox, p. 52.

45. For a lovely discussion of the significant rituals involved in women's work of food preparation, see essays from the section on "Feeding as Sacred Ritual," in Elizabeth Dodson Gray, ed., *Sacred Dimensions of Women's Experience* (Wellesley, MA: Roundtable Press, 1988), pp. 168-192.

46. James Earl Massey, *Spiritual Disciplines* (Grand Rapids, MI: Asbury Press, 1985), p. 66.

47. Roberta Bondi, *To Love as God Loves* (Philadelphia: Fortress Press, 1987), p. 76.

48. Fisher, p. 321.

Second Course: Gluttony—A Historical Digest

1. David R. Lien, Vice President for Counseling Ministries, "Insight for Living," Fullerton, California (letter of May 4, 1990).

2. Carl and LaVonne Braaten, p. 47.

3. Carl and LaVonne Braaten, p. 42.

4. Scriptural allusions in this paragraph refer to the following passages: "a glutton and a drunkard" (Mt. 11:19, Lk. 7:34); John's disciples fast while those of Jesus do not (Mt. 9:15, Mk. 2:19, Lk. 5:34); parables of the banquet (Mt. 22:1-10, Lk. 14:15-24); feeding the five thousand, the only miracle recorded by all four gospels (Mt. 14:13-21; Mk. 6:32-44; Lk. 9:10-17; Jn. 6:1-15); Matthew and Mark also tell of a feeding of four thousand (Mt. 15:32-39; Mk. 8:1-10); all four gospels tell of the Last Supper (Mt. 26; Mk. 14; Lk. 22; John 13); the resurrection appearance on the road to Emmaus (Lk. 24:30); breakfast on the beach with the disciples (John 21:1-14).

5. Scriptural allusions in this paragraph are as follows: "not by bread alone" (Mt. 4:4; Lk. 4:4); "life more than food" (Mt. 6:25, Lk. 12:22-23); Jesus' wilderness fast (Mt. 4:1-2; Mk. 1:13; Lk. 4:1-2); rich man and Lazarus (Lk. 16:19-31); feeding the poor (Mt. 25: 31-46); woes and blessings unto the full and the hungry (Lk. 6:25, 21).

6. Allusions are as follows: Acts 13:2-3; warnings against drunkenness and counsels of control (Rom. 1:24-32; Gal. 5:19-21; I Cor. 5:11; I Tim. 3:3; Titus 2:3; II Tim. 3:4; Phil. 3:19).

7. Scriptural allusions, in order, are as follows: Mark 7:18-19; I Cor. 8:8; Rom. 14:3; Col. 2:23; and I Tim. 4:2-4.

8. Fisher, *The Art of Eating*, pp. 31 and 32.

9. Originally, there were eight and not seven deadly (or capital, cardinal) sins. The restriction of the number to seven occurs in the writings of Gregory the Great. For more on the emergence and development of this tradition, see the classic historical analysis by Morton Bloomfield, *The Seven Deadly Sins* (East Lansing, MI: Michigan State College Press, 1952).

10. Herbert Musurillo, "The Problem of Ascetical Fasting in the Greek Patristic Writers," *Traditio*, vol. 12 (1956), especially pp. 24 and 49.

11. For Clement's claim, see *Stromateis* VI, ix (71), in *The Early Christian Fathers*, ed. and trans. Henry Bettenson (New York: Oxford University Press, 1969), p. 175. For the text from Basil, see Musurillo, p. 15, n. 35.

12. Musurillo quotes Abbot Nilus on p. 16 and Gregory of Nyssa on p. 40.

13. Abbot Daniel, *Apophthegmata de abbate Daniele* 4, quoted by Musurillo, p. 31; Jerome cited by William R. Mueller in "Of Obesity and Election," *Christian Century*, vol. 75 (November 26, 1958), p. 1366; Basil on "leanness," see "The Long Rules" in his collection of *Ascetical Works*,

trans. Monica Wagner (New York: Fathers of the Church, Inc., 1950), p. 273; Basil's letter *To the Young Men*, cited by Musurillo, p. 15.

14. Chrysostom, *Homilies on the Book of Acts*, cited by Musurillo, p. 15 and pp. 18–19, n. 11.

15. Chrysostom, *Adversus ebriosos*, cited by Musurillo, p. 42; Origen, *Commentary on Matthew*, cited by Musurillo, p. 38; Gregory of Nyssa, cited by Musurillo, p. 39.

16. Origen, *Homilies on Leviticus*, in Musurillo, p. 50. On the importance of complementing fasting with charity, see Bridget Ann Henisch, *Fast and Feast: Food in Medieval Society* (University Park, PA: The Pennsylvania State University Press, 1976), especially p. 29.

17. See Henisch, p. 9. Henisch cites further stories of austerity tempered by hospitality on pp. 8 and 10.

18. St. Syncletice, quoted by Miles, p. 193, n. 1.

19. Evagrius Ponticus, *The Praktikos*, trans. John Eudes Bamberger (Spencer: MA: Cistercian Publications, 1970), p. 27; Jean Cassien, *Institutions Cénobitiques*, trans. from the Latin by Jean-Claude Guy (Paris: Les Editions du Cerf, 1965), p. 205 (my translation from the French).

20. See Evagrius, *Praktikos* #16, p. 21; Basil, "On Renunciation of the World," in *Ascetical Writings*, pp. 24–25; Cassian, "Des huits principaux vices," *Conférences*, trans. from the Latin by Dom E. Pichery (Paris: Les Editions du Cerf, 1955), p. 199 (my translation from the French).

21. See Carl and LaVonne Braaten, p. 50.

22. Numerous authors note this connection between gluttony and lust. Perhaps the most graphic depiction occurs in Basil of Ancyra who writes, "As the stomach swells with food, the organs beneath it are necessarily stimulated . . . by the deeply seething humors." See Musurillo, p. 14.

23. Gregory I, *Pastoral Care*, trans. Henry Davis (Westminster, MD: The Newman Press, 1950). All subsequent page references to this work will be provided parenthetically in the text.

24. Robert Gillet, introduction to Gregory, *Morales sur Job*, trans. from the Latin by André de Gaudemaris (Paris: Editions du Cerf, 1974), p. 99.

25. Henisch, p. 16.

26. Gregory, *Morales* 30,60. See also Patrick Leigh Fermor on "Gluttony" in *The Seven Deadly Sins*, ed. by Ian Fleming (New York: William Morrow and Co., 1962), p. 38.

27. See Henisch, p. 27.

28. "The Big Business of Weight Loss," p. 4.

29. Porter, Preface to Camporesi, *Bread of Dreams*, p. 9.

30. For various treatments of the emergence of a private penitential system, see: John McNeill, *A History of the Cure of Souls* (New York: Harper and Row, 1951); John McNeill and Helena Gamer, *Medieval Handbooks of Penance: A Translation of the Principle Libri Poenitentiales and Selections from Related Documents* (New York: Columbia University Press, 1938); Pierre Payer, *Sex and the Penitentials: The Development of a Sexual Code 550-1150* (Toronto: University of Toronto Press, 1984); Thomas Tentler, *Sin and Confession on the Eve of the Reformation* (Princeton: Princeton University Press, 1977); Cyril Vogel, *Les "Libri Poenitentiales": Typologie des Sources du Moyen Age Occidental* (Turnhout, Belgium: Brepols, 1978); Oscar Watkins, *A History of Penance*, Volume 2: *The Western Church from A.D. 450 to A.D. 1215* (New York: Burt Franklin, 1961).

31. The direct quotations from various medieval penitentials are all taken from the primary documents as translated and edited by McNeill and Gamer. Page references from this source are provided parenthetically within the text.

32. For more on the differentiation between clean and unclean animals in the medieval penitentials, see Vogel, *Les "Libri Poenitentiales,"* pp. 110-111.

33. See Watkins, vol. 2, p. 769.

34. For more particulars on the life of Thomas Aquinas, see G. K. Chesterton's delightful biography, *Saint Thomas Aquinas: The Dumb Ox* (Garden City, NY: Image Books, Doubleday, 1956).

35. Thomas Aquinas, *Summa Theologica*, IaIIae, Q. 24, art. 2. From the *Summa* in three volumes, translated by Fathers of the English Dominican Province (New York: Benziger Brothers, Inc., 1947). Henceforward, references to this source will be provided parenthetically within the text. I will modify translations from the Latin to avoid exclusive language in reference to human beings.

36. There are two indispensable, complementary studies of these women: Bell, *Holy Anorexia*, and Bynum, *Holy Feast and Holy Fast*. As Bynum herself aptly analyzes the differences between the two books: "[Bell's] covers a more limited geographical area and a longer time period. His subject is abstinence, treated without reference to the positive significance of food in Christian practice. His research is more quantitative than mine. His explanatory model is psychological. Whereas Bell has been interested in women's fasting behavior, putting it into a psychological context, I have concentrated on women's use of food as symbol, putting it into a cultural context" (xiv). My own discussion of the "holy anorexics" is heavily indebted to both Bell and Bynum, and is intended merely to whet the reader's appetite for a fuller delectation of the riches of these two sources.

37. Raymond of Capua, *Legenda*, cited by Bell, pp. 27–28.

38. Catherine Benincasa, Letter of 1373 or 1374, cited by Bell, pp. 22 and 23.

39. Catherine, Dialogue, cited by Bynum, p. 174.

40. Bynum, pp. 79–80.

41. Margaret Miles, "From Ascetics to Anorexics" [a review of Bynum's *Holy Feast and Holy Fast*], *Women's Review of Books*, vol. V, no. 2 (November 1987), p. 23.

42. Bynum, p. 2. For the reference to Porter's preface to Camporesi, *Bread of Dreams*, see chapter 1, note 20, above.

43. Raymond of Capua, *Life of Catherine of Siena*, cited by Bynum, p. 168.

Third Course: The God of Thinness

1. Further page references from this source will be noted parenthetically within the text.

2. For a reproduction of the Maltese goddess and of Maud Morgan's painting, see Elinor Gadon, *The Once and Future Goddess* (New York: Harper and Row, 1989), color plates 46 and 47.

3. Brillat-Savarin, *The Physiology of Taste*, translated and annotated by M. F. K. Fisher (San Francisco: North Point Press, 1986), pp. 253, 262, and 261.

4. Cited by Anne Scott Beller in *Fat and Thin: A Natural History of Obesity* (New York: Farrar, Straus, and Giroux, 1977), p. 56.

5. See Richard Gordon, *Anorexia and Bulimia: Anatomy of a Social Epidemic* (Cambridge: Basil Blackwell, 1990), p. 77, and Seid, p. 45.

6. "Gluttony confronts a Christian pilgrim" (Walters MS 141, folio 72r, detail), reprinted with the article on "Gluttony" in the *New Catholic Encyclopedia*, vol. 6 (New York: McGraw-Hill, 1967), p. 520.

7. Cited by G. R. Owst in *Literature and Pulpit in Medieval England* (Cambridge: Cambridge University Press, 1933), p. 447.

8. On the linkages among gluttony, dyspepsia, and thinness, see Seid, pp. 68–69, as well as Schwartz, pp. 27–28, 40–43, and 185.

9. See Seid, pp. 73, 76, and 99.

10. For the materials in the preceding paragraph, see Schwartz, pp. 75 and 81, and Seid, pp. 82–83.

11. Seid, pp. 94 and 110.

12. Seid, pp. 87, 90, 95, and 106; Schwartz, pp. 168–171.

13. Seid, pp. 88, 95, 101–103; Schwartz, pp. 131–134.

14. Seid, pp. 61–70.

15. Seid, pp. 81–98.

16. The pioneer in voicing this claim is Kim Chernin; see especially *The Obsession*, pp. 96–110.

17. Wolf, *The Beauty Myth* , excerpted in *The Sunday Times [London]* (September 8, 1990), Section 8, page 1.

18. On Dublin and the MLIC, see Schwartz, pp. 154–159 and 336–338, and Seid, pp. 86 and 116–122.

19. Seid, p. 108; Schwartz, p. 252.

20. Seid, pp. 129, 151–153.

21. LaLanne quoted by Schwartz, p. 233. See also Seid, p. 107.

22. On Graham, see Schwartz, pp. 23–33; on Kellogg, pp. 183–187.

23. Seid, p. 112.

24. Quoted by Seid, p. 129.

25. *Such a Pretty Face* is, in fact, the title of a poignant and important study of *Being Fat in America*, by Marcia Millman (New York: Norton, 1980).

26. On the Manhattan study, see Kelly, "The Goddess Is Fat," in Schoenfelder and Weiser, eds., *Shadow on a Tightrope*, p. 15. See also Natalie Allon, "The Stigma of Obesity in Everyday Life," in Benjamin Wolman, ed., *Psychological Aspects of Obesity: A Handbook* (New York: Van Nostrand Reinhold, 1982), pp. 146–147.

27. Allon, p. 133.

28. Jean Mayer, *Overweight: Causes, Cost, and Control* (Englewood Cliffs, NJ: Prentice-Hall, 1968), p. 118.

29. Kelly, pp. 15–16.

30. Mayer, p. 91.

31. Sally Smith, "Sizism—One of the Last 'Safe' Prejudices," *The California NOW Activist*, vol. 5, no. 7 (July 1990), p. 1.

32. Beller, p. 11.

33. This statement and the ones following are drawn from Smith, pp. 1–2.

34. Seid, p. 159.

35. Supplement on Insurance, from *NAAFA Newsletter*, vol. 20, no. 5 (February–March 1990), p. 1.

36. Smith, p. 2.

37. Mary Suh, "A Future Up in the Air," *Ms. Magazine* (September 1989), pp. 83–84.

38. For an example of a successful law suit contesting fat discrimination under the guise of discrimination against a physical disability, see *NAAFA Newsletter*, vol. 20, no. 5 (February–March 1991), p. 1.

39. See Smith, p. 2. In addition to the state of Michigan, which Smith names as the only one in which size is a legally protected category, the state of Maryland has also been the site of a recent legal decision

determining that the "perceived handicap of obesity" is protected from discrimination under state law. See *NAAFA Newsletter*, vol. xx, no. 3 (November-December, 1990), p. 1.

40. Gordon, p. 87.

41. Veblen quoted by Gordon, p. 77.

42. Seid, p. 16.

43. Vivian Mayer, "The Questions People Ask," in Shoenfielder and Wieser, eds., *Shadow on a Tightrope*, p. 28. See also Seid, p. 226. While men of middling incomes tend to be fatter than lower income males, male executives earning the highest salary levels are expected to be lean. Among women, the inverse relation between weight and income level is uniformly consistent. See Vivian Mayer, p. 35, n. 15, and Schwartz, p. 247.

44. Schwartz, p. 249.

45. Maria Root, "Disordered Eating in Women of Color," *Sex Roles*, vol. 22, nos. 7/8 (April 1990), p. 531. Also see Gordon, p. 40.

46. Cheryl Ritenbaugh, "Obesity as a Culture-Bound Syndrome," *Culture, Medicine and Psychiatry*, vol. 6 (1982), p. 357.

47. Seid, p. 131.

48. Seid, pp. 265 and 278.

49. The actual quotation from Monique Wittig is, "But remember. Make an effort to remember. Or, failing that, invent." *Les Guérillères*, trans. David Le Vay (Boston: Beacon Press, 1971), p. 89.

50. Laura Brown (referring to a paper by M. Siever), "Fat-Oppressive Attitudes and the Feminist Therapist: Directions for Change," in Laura Brown and Esther Rothblum, eds., *Overcoming Fear of Fat* (New York: Harrington Park Press, 1989), p. 25.

51. Marcia Millman notes that fatness can either make adolescent girls appear precociously "sexy," or it can lead them to "befriend boys rather than girls, becoming 'one of the boys,' since they are not regarded by either boys or girls as 'regular' girls." She adds that "probably the most common adaptation of all is for the fat adolescent girl to take on the role of the *desexualized* but sympathetic 'listener'" (p. 77, my emphasis).

52. Allon, p. 162. Jean Mayer (*Overweight*, p. 126) reports similar findings from observations of obese and non-obese adolescent girls. The more significant variables are expenditure of calories (rather than intake), and the number of excess calories required to gain a pound (which is lower for fat people than for those of "normal" [sic] weight).

53. Marianne Ware, "To those who use 'fat' as a definitive adjective," in Shoenfielder and Wieser, eds., *Shadow on a Tightrope*, p. 22.

54. Many of these political issues are articulated in the "Fat Liberation Manifesto," by Judy Freespirit and Aldebaran, in Shoenfielder and Wieser, eds., *Shadow on a Tightrope*, pp. 52–53.

55. On "flinch value," see Nancy Barron and Barbara Hollingsworth Lear, "Ample Opportunity for Fat Women," in Brown and Rothblum, eds., *Overcoming Fear of Fat*, p. 85.

56. Ware, p. 22.

57. Brown, p. 28.

58. "Man mad at wife's weight gets 6 years in death plot," *The Virginian-Pilot* (February 7, 1990), p. A-5.

59. For a fuller treatment of various Christian weight loss programs, see Schwartz, pp. 307–310 and Seid, pp. 107 and 168. On the Overeaters Victorious program, see Marie Chapin and Neva Coyle, *Free to Be Thin* (Minneapolis: Bethany House Publishers, 1979), and Campbell, *Thin, Trim and Triumpant*, p. 15.

Fourth Course: Fruits of the Spirit

1. C. S. Lovett, *Help Lord–the Devil Wants Me Fat!*, cited by Janet Tanaka in "Will Size 22 Fit Through the Pearly Gates?" *Daughters of Sarah* (September/October 1989), p. 16.

2. Decrying the solemn secrecy characterizing so much of the gnostic cult of slenderness, Capon makes a very un-coy public admission of his weight in his book on *Health, Money, and Love* , p. 159. As a woman on her way out of the cupboard of an eating disorder, I find it appropriate at this juncture for me to make a similar admission. I stand at 5′9½″ tall (*without* those two-inch heels allowed by the Metropolitan Life Insurance Company height/weight charts). I weigh in at somewhere between 145 and 150 pounds. By most calculations, this makes me a robust figure; it does not make me fat.

I make this admission, albeit with some trepidation, for a number of reasons. First, I find myself agreeing from personal experience with the current rash of writings on shame and addiction which assert that the attempt at *hiding* is a key ingredient in promoting addictive behaviors. On the other hand, public profession/confession—for example, of my obsessions with weight and food—causes those obsessions to lose some of their power. It is a curious paradox: the more I write about my life as a binge-eater, the less frequently I find myself bingeing.

Second, as I work to break free from the power of an eating and dieting obsession, I recognize that it is important to try to see my body in a more realistic fashion. I am, indeed, a tall and broad-shouldered person, blessed with a sturdy physique and good physical condition. But I will never be slender and willowy.

Still, when I look at myself through the eyes of reason rather than obsession, when I stop bowing down before a pseudo-deity of unnatural thinness, I recognize that I do *not* need to lose another "eschatological" five pounds. To admit this to myself is nothing less than revolutionary. (It makes me begin to wonder what I will have left to hope and to work for, but those are issues for later in this chapter.)

Yet, I feel some trepidation about making this full disclosure of my size. In part, the trepidation comes from that lip-curling inner voice that whispers to me, "Who cares?" But in honesty, I imagine a number of people do. Whenever I read a book about fatness and thinness, I look to see if there is a picture of the author on the book jacket to complement or lend credence to the text . . . and I don't think I'm the only one to do this (though whether or not any of us *should* engage in such activities is another matter). In part, my trepidation roots in the general cultural dictate that women (in particular) are to lie about our ages and keep utter silence about our weights—as if these numbers couched some shameful secret about our identities. And in part, my trepidation grows out of my increasing sense of solidarity with the Size Acceptance movement. If I want to be in solidarity with people who are oppressed because of their weight, do I seem to turn traitor by the public announcement that "I am not fat"? (On the other hand, however, if I keep using the adjective "fat" of myself, at my size, do I not do an oppressive disservice to those people to whom the term more aptly applies?)

Finally, I buttress my sense of the aptness and therapeutic honesty of making public profession of my relatively "normal" weight by acknowledging the sad truth that for me to write about fat liberation as a "non-fat" person may, paradoxically, carry more weight (so to speak) than for a fat person to do so. In our fat-phobic society, for a fat person to argue about fatness as a "given" condition rather than a matter of culpable "choice" is to sound like special pleading; to hypercritical ears, it seems as though the speaker is simply making excuses for his or her "failure" to live up (or down) to the "norm." Laura Brown voices a point similar to this in her article about "Fat-Oppressive Attitudes and the Feminist Therapist." As a formerly "overweight" person writing about fat oppression in psychotherapy, she notes: "Were I still clearly a fat woman I would have encountered even more discounting and fat-oppressive responses to my work than I actually have" (p. 22). In other words, our biases against fat people are so strong that we even rob them of the opportunity to speak persuasively from their own experiences and insights about their oppression.

3. Wayne Wooley, "Indictment of Dieting—II," speech delivered to NAAFA's Tenth Anniversary Celebration on September 2, 1979, and subsequently reprinted by NAAFA (P.O. Box 188620, Sacramento, California, 95918).

4. The Kissilef, Jordan, and Levitz article from volume 2 of the *International Journal of Obesity* (1978) is summarized by Barron and Lear, p. 88.

5. Susan C. Wooley and Orland W. Wooley, "Should Obesity Be Treated At All?" in *Eating and Its Disorders*, ed. by Albert J. Stunkard and E. Stellar (New York: Raven Press, 1984), p. 185.

6. Albert J. Stunkard, "An Adoption Study of Human Obesity," *New England Journal of Medicine*, vol. 314 (1986), p. 193; and Stunkard et al., "The Body-Mass Index of Twins Who Have Been Reared Apart," *New England Journal of Medicine*, vol. 322 (1990), pp. 1483-1487. For a presentation and critique of Stunkard's findings, see Stanton Peele, Archie Brodsky, and Mary Arnold, *The Truth about Addiction and Recovery* (New York: Simon and Schuster, 1991), pp. 118-123.

7. For a summary of Bouchard's findings, see Jane Brody, "Research Lifts Blame from Many of the Obese," Science Times section of *The New York Times* (March 24, 1987), p. C-6.

8. Research of Theodore B. Van Itallie, reported by Brody, p. C-6.

9. Susan Wooley, "Indictment of Dieting—I," speech to NAAFA's Tenth Anniversary Celebration (September 2, 1979), p. 1.

10. William Bennett and Joel Gurin, *The Dieter's Dilemma: Eating Less and Weighing More* (New York: Basic Books, 1982), especially chapters 1-3.

11. For an account of Sims's research, see Bennett and Gurin, pp. 17-21.

12. See Brody, "Research Lifts Blame," p. C-6.

13. Barbara Edelstein, *The Underburner's Diet* (New York: Bantam, Doubleday, Dell, 1987), p. 48.

14. The statistic on semistarvation rations for the Dutch during Nazi occupation comes from Wolf, *The Beauty Myth* , pp. 194-195.

15. Jean Mayer, p. 6.

16. On the MLIC revision upward, see Schwartz, pp. 336-338, and Seid, p. 281. Seid (pp. 116-121) presents a fascinating account of the ways in which cultural prejudices inform scientific research in her critique of the methods by which the original MLIC height/weight tables were developed.

17. Sources for the material in this paragraph are as follows: (1) on the San Francisco longshoremen study, Seid, p. 121; (2) on the Framingham Study, Seid, pp. 280-281; (3) on Ancel Keys, Seid, p. 280, and

Wooley and Wooley, p. 186; (4) A. L. Stewart and R. H. Brook, "Effects of Being Overweight," *American Journal of Public Health*, vol. 73 (February 1983), p. 171; (5) on Reubin Andres, see Seid, p. 281 and p. 354, n. 1; (6) Eva Szekely, *Never Too Thin* (Toronto: The Women's Press, 1988), p. 168. For an excellent summary of key studies disputing the MLIC linkage between overweight and mortality, see Seid, pp. 354-356.

18. Vivian Mayer, "The Fat Illusion," in Shoenfielder and Wieser, eds., *Shadow on a Tightrope*, p. 9 and notes 13-14.

19. Vivian Mayer, "The Questions People Ask," p. 29.

20. On "restrained" versus "unrestrained" eaters, see Michael Lower and Barbara Maycock, "Restraint, Disinhibition, Hunger, and Negative Affect Eating," *Addictive Behaviors*, vol. 13 (1988), p. 369; also Jim Orford, *Excessive Appetites: A Psychological View of Addictions* (New York: John Wiley and Sons, Ltd., 1985), p. 79.

21. Jaclyn Packer, "The Role of Stigmatization in Fat People's Avoidance of Physical Exercise," in Brown and Rothblum, eds., *Overcoming Fear of Fat*, p. 54.

22. See Brody, "Research Lifts Blame," p. C-1.

23. William Bennett, "Indictment of Dieting—III," speech to the 1982 NAAFA Convention in Columbus, Ohio, p. 2.

24. Blackburn cited by Brody in "Research Lifts Blame," p. C-1.

25. Emmett presents (without advocating) these ideas in a chapter on "Further Trends," in his *Theory and Treatment of Anorexia Nervosa and Bulimia*, pp. 305-306.

26. For elaboration and critique of the disease model of alcoholism, see especially Herbert Fingarette, *Heavy Drinking: The Myth of Alcoholism as a Disease* (Berkeley: University of California Press, 1988). For presentation of the position that "some foods can be as addictive as cocaine or alcohol," see Father Joseph Martin, Foreword to *Food Addiction*, p. ix.

27. For examples of the moral model, see Orford, *Excessive Appetites*, and Peele et al., *The Truth About Addiction and Recovery*.

28. Peele et al., p. 109.

29. I include the word "medical" in quotation marks, because even this term seems to suggest that there is something pathological about fatness—that it is not simply a physiological variation, but a disease. Given data presented earlier in this chapter, I disagree with such an assessment. Rather, I agree with psychoanalyst D. H. Ingram, who states: "It is not clear that obesity is a major determinant of impaired physical or emotional health. Rather, the medical treatment of obesity seems to stem from the need to justify an intensely negative cultural bias." Quoted by Allon, p. 166.

30. Peele et al., p. 112.

31. Gloria Arenson, *A Substance Called Food* (Blue Ridge Summit, PA: TAB Books, Inc., 1989 [second edition]), p. 91.

32. Peele et al., p. 112.

33. William Davis, Epilogue to Bell, *Holy Anorexia*, pp. 189-190. On the correlational, rather than causal, relationship between bulimia and depression, see also Szekely, p. 35.

34. For a fuller discussion of anorexia nervosa as a "syndrome" rather than an illness, see Richard Green and John Rau, "The Use of Diphenyl-hydantoin in Compulsive Eating Disorders," in *Anorexia Nervosa*, ed. R. A. Vigersky (New York: Raven Press, 1977), p. 381. On the concept of "culture-bound syndromes," see Ritenbaugh, pp. 347-361; and Gordon, pp. 6-11.

35. On "maturing out" of addictive behaviors, see Fingarette, pp. 72 and 110, and Orford, pp. 258-259.

36. Lloyd Steffen, "Rethinking Drinking: The Moral Context," *The Christian Century* (July 19-26, 1989), p. 685.

37. For a fuller treatment of the criteria by which gluttony is assessed as sinful, see chapter two (especially pages 69-71 and 77-78).

38. See chapter one, note 42, above.

39. Two different sorts of comments seem in order here. First, in a world plagued by starvation, it may seem obscene to talk about throwing food away. It is certainly true that the relatively affluent among us waste outrageous amounts of money—whether on junk food or on diet food—which could be fruitfully used toward the alleviation of world hunger. However, the point I am making here is that once the food has been purchased, the chronic overeater would do better to put "left-overs" into a dumpster than into his or her mouth. A person who feels consistently overstuffed and self-loathing saps the energies needed for social activism. On the other hand, a person who feels healthy and powerful over food may find in that strength the further impetus to engage in work on hunger and other justice issues.

Second, there are a variety of books which offer helpful tips for discovering new behaviors to replace the bad habits of addictions. Two of the more recent titles are Peele et al., *The Truth about Addiction and Recovery*; and Frank Minirth, Paul Meier, Robert Hemfelt, and Sharon Sneed, *Love Hunger: Recovery from Food Addiction* (Nashville: Thomas Nelson Publishers, 1990). Both these books do tend to conflate overcoming an eating compulsion with going on a diet and to assume that "overweight" and "overeating" are synonymous. Otherwise, however, they suggest a variety of useful strategies for developing constructive coping skills.

40. On the presumed "magic" of foods and dietary rituals, note the observations of James Rosen and Harold Leitenberg on "Eating Behavior in Bulimia Nervosa," in Timothy Walsh, ed., *Eating Behavior in Eating Disorders* (Washington, D.C.: American Psychiatric Press, 1988), p. 166. They explain that careful study of bulimics shows "binge" episodes generally to be less frequent and caloric than they are reported to have been, and that the distress over these episodes is not related to the actual amount of food consumed, but rather to the perception that *certain foods are in themselves* "excessive and dangerously fattening": "A wide variety of foods of normal quantity are considered unsafe, repulsive, and fattening. Vomiting is the magic ritual that [bulimics] believe protects them from these terrifying consequences."

41. Brian W. Grant, *From Sin to Wholeness* (Philadelphia: Westminster, 1982), pp. 37–38.

42. J. Scott Mizes and Robert C. Klesges, "Validity, Reliability, and Factor Structure of the Anorectic Cognitions Questionnaire," in *Addictive Behaviors*, vol. 14, no. 5 (1988), p. 589.

43. The dynamics of anorexia are different from this. While not knowing them from personal experience, I gather from reading the literature and listening to students and workshop participants who are recovering anorexics that the desire felt in anorexia is that of prolonging the experience of hunger as long as possible, because the yawning, empty feeling produces a surge of power, a proud sense of control.

44. Terence Sandbek, *The Deadly Diet: Recovering from Anorexia and Bulimia* (Oakland, California: New Harbinger Publications, 1986), p. 67.

45. On restrained and unrestrained eating, see note 20 above.

46. For more on "caloric Pelagianism," see my article "Confessions of a Glutton," *The Christian Century* (10/25/89), p. 957.

47. Jane Hirschmann and Carol Munter, *Overcoming Overeating* (New York: Fawcett Columbine, 1988); Marion Bilich, *Weight Loss from the Inside Out: Help for the Compulsive Eater* (New York: Harper and Row, 1983); Susan Kano, *Making Peace with Food: Freeing Yourself from the Diet/Weight Obsession* (New York: Harper and Row, 1989); Orbach, *Fat Is a Feminist Issue, II*; Geneen Roth, *Breaking Free from Compulsive Eating* (New York: New American Library, 1984).

48. Hirschmann and Munter, p. 117.

49. See chapter one, note 33, above.

50. May, *Addiction and Grace*, p. 31.

51. Geneen Roth, "Days Alone Come Down to This," in *Feeding the Hungry Heart*, pp. 99–100.

Digestif: Daily Graces

1. Capon, *The Supper of the Lamb*, pp. 27–28.